The Good Side
of Memory

MARTY MATTHEWS

The Good Side of Memory

Cover image licensed through Shutterstock.com

Cover designed by Faleena Hopkins

This is a work of fiction. Names, characters, businesses, places, events and incidents are either the products of the author's imagination or are used in a fictitious manner. Any resemblance to actual persons, living or dead, or actual events is purely coincidental.

No part of this book may be reproduced, or stored in a retrieval system, or transmitted in any form or by any means, electronic, mechanical, photocopying, recording, or otherwise, without the express written permission of the publisher.

Copyright © 2016 Marty Matthews
All rights reserved.

ISBN-13: 978-1539164371

ISBN-10: 1539164373

From The Author

Memories, from time to time, are what keep us going. Could be good memories, bad memories, sad memories, happy memories – everyone can relate to that! We all have them, we all talk about them, and, really, we all need them. Because of that need, I wanted to put in writing the memories that I have, and ones that I can share, as a pre-teen and teen in the early 1960s while living on Lenox Avenue in Norfolk, Virginia. In my entire life spanning six decades, the memories encompassing those four years – 1960 - 1964 -- are my best, ones that still make me smile when I think of them.

I am sure many others have those same kinds of special memories – the boy next door, a very best friend, and innocent times of simple fun. Because I wanted to hear from others and learn about their special memories of a time long ago, I reached out to those who were actually my special people living where I did during those years as well as to others with whom I am not even acquainted. All of them told me about their own youth and their own memories that have lasted a lifetime for them too. So many were similar to mine, yet many were also quite different; nevertheless, the memories for them, as they were for me, maintained the innocence and fun of their youth. <u>The Good Side of Memory</u> entails the early 1960s, the years which are my memories, and are your memories too. It was a time that was simple, that was fun, and that was enjoyed by all.

So sit back, put your mind on hold, and enjoy memories that we all can share! The names can be changed to become your names, and the places and events can become your places and events. Just as Jan Hodgson from Tennessee said, "I have wonderful memories of my own Lenox Avenue – only it was called Washington Road on Missionary Ridge in Chattanooga, Tennessee." As Jan did, take time to reminisce, to laugh, perhaps shed a tear or two, but enjoy! That's what <u>The Good Side of Memory</u> is for – enjoyment!

Acknowledgements

Thank you, Donna Liverett and Jon Fye, for proofing my manuscript with your suggestions, insertions, and deletions. I never can do it without you! Also thank you both for sharing your own memories in this book.

A special thank you to my husband, Fred Matthews, who has always been supportive through every book I write. I especially thank him for sharing his own memories on these pages and making me laugh through his stories.

As always, a grateful thank you to Faleena Hopkins, my consultant, who puts my books together for publishing. Her creativeness is exemplary, and I am more amazed at her skills with each book, this one being no exception.

Marty Matthews

Memory Makers

Thank you so much for those of you who reached out to share your memories. I'm listing below your names and places at the time of each of your memories. Some of you did not want your entire name listed; therefore, for those, I only list the first names and last initial:

- Fred Matthews – Hanahan, South Carolina
- Bubba Williams – Norfolk, Virginia
- Paula Rapisardi O'Connor – Norfolk, Virginia
- David Lindhjem – Norfolk, Virginia
- Kathy Steenson – Miami, Florida
- Kathy Schlegel – York, Pennsylvania
- Brenda Fye – Mitchell, Indiana
- Jon Fye – Bedford, Indiana
- Dianne G. – Clarksville, Tennessee
- Mary Lou Graham – Nashville, Tennessee
- Mary Lou S. – Clarksville, Tennessee

- Kim Matthews – Ocean City, New Jersey
- Elaine Rose – Roseburg, Oregon
- Carolyn Martin – Okinawa, Japan
- Lynn E. – Franklin, Indiana
- Larry Velasquez – Key West, Florida
- Chris Hoffman – Paradise, California
- Carol Cole – Nashville, Tennessee
- Jan Hodgson – Chattanooga, Tennessee
- Lali Alfonso – Key West, Florida
- Donna Liverett – Knoxville, Tennessee

The Good Side of Memory

I

The House and the School

Two words – Lenox Avenue. They evoke a plethora of memories and bring a smile to my lips every time I hear them, see them, or write them. Lenox Avenue. A simple street with small, practical houses on each side of the road, but a street nevertheless that floods my soul with memories. I have recently stood on that street fifty years after I first arrived, closed my eyes, and let the memories come. A breeze whispered, a voice tantalized, a slow-moving car rumbled. Oh yes, opening my eyes, I could still remember as if it were yesterday. Memories of a special house, special people, and a special fun that is not seen in the different era of 2016.

How can the name of a street do so much? It's like hearing a song and instantly, you are back in the time when it played and when you enjoyed every nuance of that period. It's like smelling a smell that makes you breathe deeper and summon a time when you can almost open your mouth and taste the aroma that took you back in time. It's like feeling a light breeze that blows as you walk, making you close your eyes and picture yourself in a past in which you're reliving again – a déjà vu. It's like seeing a picture, a reminder, having you close your eyes and think, "That really takes me back."

Yes, the words, Lenox Avenue does all that for me and more. Those of us that lived on that short block of Lenox Avenue in the 1960s can also probably relate to those two words evoking those special memories. But I imagine there are many of you who can elicit those same feelings with your two words of your own street, your own city, your own special place, just like Jan did with her Washington Road in Chattanooga, Tennessee. For me, there are no two words – Lenox Avenue -- that bring such fond memories in the relative short time that I spent there, which was approximately four years.

It began in 1960 when my parents decided they were tired of renting – I assume they were tired of renting because I had heard my dad say often enough to my mother that all the money they had paid to landlords went "right down the tubes." They didn't actually say the words to me, but it seems obvious when I heard him talk to my mother and think of how our move to Lenox Avenue came about. To rent or not to rent, that seemed to be the statement at hand. Obviously, it was not to rent and they decided to take the plunge and purchase their first home. A home all of their own.

As a girl of ten years old, I really had no say in the matter except to go with my parents whenever they looked at various homes. I voiced my opinion about every house at which we looked, but it really fell on deaf ears. My dad was one that adhered to the adage that children should really be seen and not heard. Oh, he may have listened to what I said while we scouted possible homes, but he would have patted my shoulder had I said anything about what I did or didn't like and moved on to the next house at his own discretion. My mother had more of a say than I did, and I heard them talking about each house as they looked, but it was really my dad's decision.

I can remember various houses we saw, and ones I really liked – the ones with the best bedroom in which I would call my own. Of course, my bedroom was the least of my parents' thoughts when it came to the buying of our first house. Consequently, I sighed and kept looking with them.

As we traipsed from house to house, we finally came to Lenox Avenue and saw the house. THE house! It was a quiet street – Lenox Avenue – neatly kept yards, no abandoned toys, no cars racing up and down the street. It was quiet without too many cars because only the people living in that first block where THE house was located would have a need to travel there. Other entrances onto Lenox Avenue were in every block thereafter; therefore, the first block was rather quiet.

Getting out of the car, I saw her riding by on her bicycle, brown, curly hair flowing behind her. I watched as she rode on down Lenox Avenue and turned the corner. As we walked up the sidewalk to the porch of the house I asked my parents, "Did you see that girl? I think she's my age!"

My mother turned to me and said, "What girl?"

"The girl on the bicycle," I pointed down the road, but she was no longer visible.

My dad shook his head, indicating he saw no one; his thoughts were elsewhere – certainly not on a girl on a bicycle. He was looking at every aspect of the house from the outside: the yard – front and back – the bushes, trees, and the beautiful flower garden nestled between the house and the house next door. Of course, they didn't realize then, but they would see "that girl" over the next forty years – through her growing adult years, attending her wedding (I was in the wedding – the matron of honor), meeting her three children, and grieving the loss of her father. In 1960, though, it was, "What girl?" I sighed again and followed my parents into the house.

I believe my parents and I were mesmerized as soon as we walked inside the house. It seemed huge in comparison to the previous houses we had rented; therefore, the first asset I visualized as I looked around the living room was a good sized bedroom for me. Even better, it was a two-story house, which I had never lived in. I imagined running up the stairs and throwing open the door to my bedroom – OR running up the stairs and shutting the door to my bedroom for privacy! Privacy on a different floor – all by myself -- while my parents watched TV or had people over for dinner. Wow! Things could not be better. This had to be the house!

Of course, while I had visions of my room and my privacy, my parents were interested in the neighborhood, schools, the area as to how close it was to where my father worked, but mainly they were interested in the house itself.

"It's unique," words my father said until the day he passed away in the year 2000.

I think of that now and realize that Lenox Avenue had a huge impact on him too. He had mentioned the house on more than one occasion once we had moved from it in 1964. In fact, David Lindhjem, who lived two streets over from Lenox Avenue and became a good friend, wrote to me once we moved and said, "I think your parents would have been far ahead of the game if they had rented your house, then came back to live in it later." I mentioned that to my dad years later when he talked of the house, and he said David had had the right idea, and he wished that he, himself, had thought that too. Of course, 20/20, water under the bridge, etc. etc. Didn't happen that way.

The house was unique in that it had a curved wall between the living room and dining room with a closet, on the other side of the curved wall, that could be entered into in two different doorways in two different rooms. My parents found that fascinating. They also liked the fireplace sitting in the living room, which we had never had in any of our rentals as well as a huge picture window which overlooked the golf course just past our backyard.

Additionally, the house had something none of the other houses had on Lenox Avenue – a half bathroom. Most houses at that time had only one bathroom, and it wasn't in the master bedroom – if there were a master bedroom back then. The bathroom was usually in the hallway near all of the bedrooms – definitely two, possibly three -- and everyone shared the bathroom at various times. Our half bathroom was downstairs on the main floor, and it was a novelty for all of us – "unique!"

Of course, once seeing it, I still couldn't wait to call the bedroom upstairs my own. To me it was huge! I had the main bedroom itself, which was where I would actually sleep, but then there was also a heavy accordion folding, moveable "wall" that could be completely pushed back between my bedroom and another smaller room. That afforded me to have my bedroom as well as the room on the other side of the accordion wall all to myself! I had the entire width of that part of the house for a bedroom, and I loved it! In my main bedroom, I had windows near my bed that faced out over the golf course; in my other room, I had a window that faced out on Lenox Avenue. Oh, yes, I was in heaven over my room.

My parents had chosen the bedroom for themselves which was just slightly down the hall from me. It was smaller than the room I had – especially with my added smaller room with the accordion wall pushed all the way back – but their room was beside the upstairs bathroom. A plus for them, not really a care for me.

Something that my parents were eager to have (and perhaps sealed the deal for my father) was what was called in 1960 – an integral garage. The garage was a part of the house – not a detached unit in which one parked the car, shut the garage door, and then walked to the house. No, this garage was part of the house in which one parked, shut the garage door, and walked right into the house through the first door. Incidentally, there were no garage door openers. Whether one opened the detached garage door or the integral garage door, the garage door still had to be opened manually and shut manually. What we find in 2016 to be routine and in just about every garage and home, the integral garage was a novel idea in 1960.

Not every home had an integral garage, a rounded wall, or even a bathroom in the early 1960s. Donna Liverett of Tennessee said, "We lived in railroad housing and there was no insulation in/on the walls. You could see through the walls where the planks of wood met. During the winter snowstorms, it literally snowed in the house. We had a sink in the kitchen, but that was the only indoor plumbing we had. If you had to use the bathroom, you did so either in the outhouse or in the chamber pot (kept under the bed and emptied in the outhouse daily). Mom told me she remembers it being so cold that the faucet in the sink froze one winter, broke off from the pipe, and fell into the sink! We were so poor, but we didn't know it because we were so rich in love."

Sometime thereafter, the deal was sealed, and we moved to Lenox Avenue. I still hadn't met "that girl" but I watched her on numerous occasions riding up and down Lenox Avenue on her bicycle. I also rode my bicycle up and down Lenox Avenue, at times passing her on the way. We checked each other out as we rode by, but not a word was spoken. Finally after a couple of more days like that, we actually broke the ice and introduced ourselves. From then on – an inseparable twosome!

One could look back to the 1960s and see quite different living conditions in our perfect house (perfect -- from my perspective) on Lenox Avenue. We, along with everyone else, did not have central air conditioning. I'm not sure if anyone had air conditioning window units either at that time – I know we didn't. We did have a window fan for those long, hot summer months, which my father placed in the window of the smaller room (accordion room) next to my big bedroom. Of course when the window fan went in the window, there was no shutting the bedroom doors – either in my big bedroom or the smaller room -- for privacy!

"It will stop the proper flow of air," my dad said over and over. "When the fan is turned on, you keep your bedroom doors opened."

And my dad, using his mathematical mind and probably his slide rule, said once the fan was turned on to the "out" position, all windows in the house, upstairs and downstairs, had to be up six inches – no more, no less. He said it created the perfect breeze. One might raise eyebrows questioning that mathematical philosophy, but I honestly don't remember the days or nights being too hot, so perhaps he was exactly right. However, Paula Rapisardi O'Connor – "the girl"-- remembers that her mother used to put a bowl of cool water with a wash cloth in it by her bed at night. If she awoke in the middle of the night and was too hot, she could wring out the rag and put it on her face.

Another difference was the telephone – providing families had one. We actually had TWO phones, one for upstairs and one for downstairs. Both were rotary dials and the standard black color graced our phone upstairs. My dad wanted a beige one for our kitchen – it was a wall phone – so it wouldn't look so hideous against the white walls. Incidentally, he painted the kitchen blue later on, and the beige wall phone looked as good on it as on the white wall. My dad also painted all the rooms in the house once we moved in. Of course, that was after removing all the wallpaper – with a scraper and buckets of water. Wallpaper, at that time, was nothing like it is today (if it is still used), and it was a tedious chore to remove.

Of course, what I really liked about the upstairs phone – the cord was long enough (from wall to phone) that I could pull the phone in my room, shut the door (providing it wasn't summer, and the breeze was blowing perfectly through raised six inch windows), and I had my very own phone in my room! Lots of privacy for me! Some people, such as Jon Fye of Indiana, reminded me, that a good many phones had party lines. That meant, at any one given time, someone could pick up the telephone receiver to make a call and another person could possibly already be talking on the other end. If so, the receiver had to be hung up, and it became a waiting game. The one trying to make the call would pick up the receiver every few minutes to check and see if the other party was finished talking. At times it could be unpleasant to have to wait because some conversations were quite lengthy! And we won't even go into no privacy – if someone on the other end decided to "listen in" to your conversation.

Our family paid extra for a private line because my parents didn't want the party line. Since my dad was in the Navy, he received calls every so often and he couldn't afford to miss them because someone was on the other line; hence, we had a private line and not a party line. One last memory about the phone – all telephone numbers consisted of letters and numbers. Evidently, the first two letters were for a certain area, then the last five numbers were people's specific telephone numbers. While I don't remember my own number, I still remember (fifty years later) the number for the boy next door (who moved in two years after we did) -- JU 7-0604. What can I say? At the ripe age of 13, I was smitten and in love!

Incidentally, in 1963, the touch-tone telephones were introduced and from that time on, the phone changed dramatically time and time again from the huge, black, rotary dial to what we have today.

Also different in that era, no one used their clothes dryers (if they had one) in the summer as all hung the wash outside to dry. The clothes hung on at least three lines (spaced about one foot apart), stretched between two metal "T" poles, probably about twenty or more feet apart -- just like that, too, in the shape of a "T". Probably every back yard had clothes lines – it would really seem unnatural back then not to have clothes lines. Most importantly, before hanging out the clothes, the lines had to be cleaned off with a rag. It was as simple as wrapping a rag around each line and walking from one end of the line to the other. Nobody wanted to hang clothes on a line that had been the recipient of bird droppings!

I remember how wonderful the sheets smelled after bringing them in from being outside and from blowing in the wind. And they just had that special smell when crawling in between them at night that only hanging them outside elicits – bringing forth a huge inhaled breath and sigh. Incidentally, my mother was a stickler about what neighbors thought, so when we hung our clothes, sheets, and towels outside, everything had to be in order on the clothes line. For clothes – all pants together, all blouses together, all undergarments together. For the sheets – flat sheets and fitted sheets together, pillow cases next. Towels – Bath towels together, hand towels together, and wash cloths together. Everything had to be in order. I smile now as I think about it because I never noticed how anyone hung their clothes on the line, and I wonder if any other neighbors did as my mother thought they might.

Of course, once clothes were hung outside, they were brought inside with massive wrinkles in them! That meant plenty of ironing to do! My mother, and I'm sure many others too, had a sprinkler bottle. Possibly, the sprinkler bottles could be "store bought," but most everyone – including our family – fashioned them to their own liking. Ours was a Coke bottle with a little top on it with holes in the top. I don't remember how the top fitted on the Coke bottle, but I'm sure my mother had fashioned it perfectly. Water was put in the Coke bottle, and viola! The clothes would be sprinkled with as much water as one desired. At the time of sprinkling, Mother took each piece of clothing, laid it out on the kitchen table – that would be a Formica table -- sprinkled both sides of the clothes, folded them over once, then rolled them up. Once they were sprinkled, folded, and rolled, they went into the freezer. When she decided to iron, clothes would come out of the freezer, be unfolded, and would be ironed. Beautiful, perfectly ironed clothes with not one wrinkle. No starch was needed – just sprinkling, rolling, and freezing! Another note about ironing – we ironed just about everything, including under garments and pillow cases. Mother's comment about ironing pillow cases: "If you don't iron your pillow cases, you're lazy!" As an adult, I didn't take that to heart as I never ironed pillow cases or under garments.

The kitchen was somewhat different in the 1960s than it is today in 2016. My parents perked their coffee in a percolator, using a metal holder on the inside (it was removable) to hold the coffee – no filters were on the market at that time. Mother mixed everything with a hand beater, but I believe she did get an electric one not long after we moved to Lenox. There were no non-stick pots and pans – it was cast iron or aluminum. The cast iron skillet was a definite staple in every house, and my mother used it practically every night – especially for frying with grease/lard. (More about grease later). The heavy, thick aluminum pots were also a mainstay; in fact, she still had the same set when she passed away in 2000.

Obviously, no ice makers were found on the outside or inside of refrigerators. Metal ice trays were purchased and were used for the ice. And yes, the ice box was no longer the norm, and everyone had refrigerators – the ice man no longer cometh! A short note about ice trays! One learned quite fast that a tongue was never to be "licked" on the metal trays after they had been frozen and in the freezer! It was just like in the movie "A Christmas Story" when the little boy put his tongue on the flag pole in the dead of winter, and it stuck! Trust me, I was only eight years old when I stuck my tongue to the metal tray, and I never did it again! Despite the hot water (trying to dislodge my tongue) parts of the first layer of my tongue was still on the back of the metal ice cube tray!

While microwave ovens were patented in 1945, they did not find their way into homes until about 1967. Nothing could be nuked – everything was made and cooked from "scratch." Other small appliances were on the scene (toasters, some blenders, etc.) with the exception of the electric can opener.

Milk lasted for quite some time without going sour since most milk that was purchased in the store was in waxed cartons (1/2 gallon size) and no light could penetrate it. Of course the milk in glass bottles, if it was delivered to homes, lasted a good while too. Paula and her family had their milk delivered in glass bottles, and I always wanted the milkman to stop at our house so we could have the milk in the bottles too – I thought her milk tasted better. At delivery time, the milkman brought the milk to the door and set the bottles (usually six bottles in a container) on the stoop. After all the bottles were empty, and the family had enjoyed good, fresh milk, they would set the empty bottles and container back out on the stoop for the next time the milkman came to pick up and drop off the milk. It was all whole milk, too. I had never heard of skim milk or one and two percent milk back in the 1960s.

Bread was in somewhat thick bags that people

folded (rolled) up after opening. No ties for convenience or dates indicating freshness of the bread. Like the milk, it, too, seemed to last longer than the bread does today. Also, I can only remember white bread and not the many varieties that are found in the stores today. Perhaps there was wheat bread, but our family only bought white bread. And the slices were far thicker than they are today. When sandwiches were made for lunches to be carried to work or school, they were wrapped in waxed paper. There were no baggies or such as we have in 2016. There was Tupperware, though, which always kept sandwiches and everything else fresh. Incidentally, Tupperware was quite sturdy and held up well. I still have and use the cereal bowls my mother purchased when she went to one of the home Tupperware parties over fifty years ago.

Canisters sat on the kitchen cabinets (containing flour, sugar, coffee) and always boasted a grease canister, which meant every time any type of grease was left over after cooking in a pan or cast iron skillet, it was poured into the canister. When cooking vegetables and the like, a spoonful of grease was taken out of the canister and cooked with the vegetables. I think back today and can only imagine how old some of that grease was in the canisters. Does anyone remember having stomach problems??

Dishwashers did not grace the kitchens of the 1960s. Moms and daughters were the dishwashers – I know from experience! Nevertheless, Paula's Mother was the first on our block to get a dishwasher, and we were all impressed. I believe it was a gift from Paula's Dad, and everyone had to go to her house and check it out! I tried to convince my dad that we needed one, but he couldn't be so convinced and, consequently, I continued to wash and dry dishes with my mom.

Freezers were on the top half or bottom half of the refrigerators unless one had a free standing freezer. Whichever one a family had, it had to be defrosted, which was quite a chore. Depending on how thick the ice was on the shelves (if you had waited way too long to defrost!), it had to be chipped off with a knife or some type of utensil like that. Obviously, before doing so, everything had to be taken out of the freezer. Once the chipping was finished, the ice and water was wiped off the freezer shelves – catch the mess with newspapers or pans on the floor – everything was then put back into the freezer until the next time. Another easier method was setting containers of hot water inside the freezer to defrost it. Again, though, removal of items and wiping up the water was a must.

Ovens were far more difficult to clean if left too long without a good scouring. It was a Brillo pad, rinsing/dumping water, and lots of elbow grease to get it cleaned. Obviously, the invention of oven cleaner – spray on, wipe off – was heaven when it appeared in the stores. Also, many people used aluminum foil in the bottom of the oven to catch drips so that it could be thrown away when the foil became too dirty. New foil replaced it, and the process started again.

Shopping for food was quite different in that there was less to choose from; plus, there really were no big supermarket places – just mom and pop places and small chain stores. While in 2016, one can walk down aisles and see many varieties of the same type of thing such as cereals, vegetables, cookies; in 1960, one would find just a handful of those same items.

Perhaps five different brands of cereals, a few types of cookies, a variety or two of vegetables. I must add here, though, the food tasted wonderful and since most everyone cooked everything, no preservatives abounded as they do today.

Something found in just about every house in the 1960s would have been the green stamps, Top Value stamps, or some other stamps relevant to a particular grocery store. Certain stores gave green stamps to customers, and the number of stamps given depended on how much money the customer spent. My mother realized quickly the stores with the green stamps charged more for the food than the stores that did not offer the stamps. At any rate, if we happened to shop at one of the stores offering the stamps, we collected those stamps, and pasted them into books that were given out by the same stores. Then the filled books were redeemed at a redemption store that housed appliances, toys, and odds and ends, everything that you could "buy" with the books of stamps. Green stamps or other types of stamps were a popular selling point in the 1960s.

One other event with stores that is not prevalent

in 2016 is keeping a tab of items and a bill presented later. As Jon said, "My dad sent me to the grocery store, like a mom/pop place, and I would tell the owner, 'My dad said to put it on his tab.' We could do this because the store was across the alley and the owner knew my dad. Incidentally, I loved black licorice, until the doctors said it contributed to Dad's death!" Jon, I hated to hear that statement because I also love black licorice and eat it whenever I get the chance! I believe I may be the only one to do so within my family, though, and with my friends as well!

Also from stores, only brown paper bags were used for purchases – no plastic. Of course the paper bags were recycled for the use of trash bags and anything one desired rather than buying brown wrapping paper at the store. My father always recycled by using the brown paper bags for mailing packages, along with mailing twine in which was tied around the package to hold everything together firm!.

The bags could also have been used for lawn clippings, weeds, grass, etc. And what did the man of the houschold use for cutting the grass? Not the zero-turn lawn mower of 2016, but a manual push mower with rotary blades. Step, push! Step, push! It was difficult, hard work! Is it any wonder the 1960s didn't really boast of gyms for exercise?

Lastly – durability! Everything was made differently those five decades ago, and so much lasted longer than it does now. Good examples sit right in my own home in 2016: mahogany living room furniture purchased in Hawaii in 1955; dining room furniture purchased while on Lenox Avenue in 1961; and a rocking chair given to my dad from our neighbor next door – it had belonged to HER mother (and I considered our neighbor old at the time). The mahogany furniture has no scratches on it despite countless moves across the ocean twice and through the United States; the dining room furniture has minimal scratches but are not visible; and the rocking chair looks just like it did when my dad refinished it. Durability! I can't imagine anything lasting as long as these items have – and I cherish them!

****

Schools were generally located in various neighborhoods, but kids did have to walk or ride a bus occasionally to a school that was a mile or so farther from a neighborhood. The elementary school I attended (1st grade – 7th grade) was a bit of a distance from our house when we moved to Lenox Avenue. Previously, it had been across the street from my family and me. When we moved, though, a girlfriend from another neighborhood and I rode our bikes to and from that school. It was also the same when I started junior high school (8th grade and 9th grade), but typically we walked and stopped riding our bikes.

Riding a bus was "not necessary" my parents told me – get out in the elements and walk. Whether it rained or snowed, I walked. Lynn E. of Indiana agreed – we walked whether it was hot or cold outside. "I lived over a mile from the high school and there wasn't a wind chill factor…they hadn't figured that out yet. It was a different world back then. It's a wonder someone didn't have frost bite." Paying for and riding the bus was not a luxury for me and probably not for her either. Perhaps we didn't live quite far enough for the school bus to come by or there may not have been a school bus – I honestly don't remember. If there were a school bus, I never rode one. Paula and I talked about the school buses when I recently asked her about them, and she said her school gave tickets for riding the city bus in the event a student lived too far to walk. The bus would be on the regular city bus route, and students would pay with the tickets they had purchased earlier. Evidently my school was closer than hers because I knew nothing about the tickets. Neither of us, though, remembered seeing school buses come into our neighborhoods.

During the 1960s, all girls wore dresses to school – no jeans, pants, or shorts. The boys wore a type of pants such as khakis – not jeans – and their shirt tails were always tucked inside their pants. Lynn said at any given time, a girl would have to kneel to the floor, and if her dress or skirt hem did not touch the floor, she was sent home to change her dress/skirt into something "more appropriate" and longer.

Back packs were not on the market at that time, but we did carry book bags in our hands if we so desired. Otherwise, the books were carried in our arms. Donna said on her walks to and from school, with no book bag, her arms were "screaming by the time I got home." Also, according to my husband, Fred, who grew up in South Carolina, books were wrapped with brown wrapping paper once each student received his or hers at the beginning of the school year, which saved wear and tear on the books. This brown paper, in many cases, was the recycled brown paper bags one used from grocery stores in which food was carried. Like Fred's school, I believe our school also had the students wrap books.

A big difference in school classrooms were the number of students. There were generally thirty to thirty-five students in each one. BUT the teacher maintained control, the students respected that teacher, and each class progressed nicely throughout the day. There were incidents, of course, and spankings – usually done by the principal – were meted out to the offenders. These incidents were usually talking in the back of the class room – heaven forbid if a student talked back to the teacher, which was a major infraction – acting out in the classroom and getting out of the seat, or continual chewing gum in the class room. There were others, but those come to mind instantly.

Jon also recalled, "Teachers not understanding boys not developing as fast as girls. I was enrolled in September just passed the cut off date, so I was mostly the youngest and smallest boy in class. I could not read as well as the other kids in class. The teacher in third grade got so frustrated that she took me out in the hallway and spanked me. I got a bad report on my progress card and the teachers never allowed me to be on the honor roll – not once in grade school."

I never witnessed a spanking and was terrified I might receive one; hence, I never did anything (except talk to my seat mate when I could get away with it) that would warrant my teacher giving me one. I do remember boys having to go to the principal for a spanking, but I never remember any of the girls having to do so.

Something that had just come upon the scene in the classrooms was science on TV. I don't believe it was found in the upper grades, but in elementary school, we watched about fifteen minutes of a science program then generally had questions to answer about the program, or we took a quiz about the program. We still had science books and the teacher taught science, but the TV programs were enhancements to go along with the lessons.

Only chalk boards were used – no dry erase boards existed; mimeograph copies for tests were used – Xerox copies were not in the schools. Fred specifically remembers and liked the smell of the test paper when the teacher gave it to him after it had been mimeographed. I remember many times, myself, sniffing the test when the teacher handed it to me. Only pencils were used – no pens were allowed. However, even though my desk top had an inkwell, which would have held a bottle full of ink for filling fountain pens of long ago, we had now progressed to ball point pens (to be used at home).

There are fire drills now in schools, and we had them also in the 1960s; however, we also had bomb drills. At my school and others like it, when the bomb drill sounded over the loudspeaker, everyone jumped under their desks. Desks were small (approximately twenty-four inches or so) tables – usually the top lifted up and items could be put inside the desk – attached to a chair. Some desks, though, had chairs that weren't attached, and I believe that depended on the grade level of the student. In Fred's school, when the bomb drill sounded, his classmates were instructed to assemble in the hallway, sit down, and put a book over their heads. Each state was different, but bomb drills were fairly routine.

Regarding walking to school – my mother also walked to her job at the library. Since our family, and all of the families on Lenox Avenue, had only one car, my mother and I walked to our destinations. My dad had to go to work far earlier and much farther than I did for my school or Mother did for her work, so he drove the only car for the family. Paula's family had only one car, which her father also drove to work; however, her mother didn't need a car since she didn't know how to drive at all. Her entire life was devoid of a driver's license, and she walked everywhere she needed to go.

It was a time when no one was afraid to be alone on the streets, whether you were a child or whether you were an adult. Of course, obvious precautions would have been made regarding strangers, but it wasn't something that was drilled into our heads like it is in 2016. When Paula walked to her school at the start of her education – the Catholic elementary school – she was only six years old. We knew where to go, and we went to our destination without another thought. When moving to Lenox Avenue, I was ten years old, and I rode my bike to a friend's house, then she and I would ride to the elementary school together. When I entered the junior high school, I walked to a different friend's house – the first friend having moved away as her father was in the Navy also – and we walked to the school together. Being afraid to walk never entered our minds. What did enter our minds was what did our hair look like when we arrived at school? If it was hot, hair would have frizzed or gone straight from perspiration. If it were cold, windy, or snowy, hair took on an entirely different look. First on the agenda when entering school – head to the restroom and check out the hairdo! Whatever the case may be with walking or riding bicycles, what we would consider frightening in walking/riding the streets alone today was the norm in the 1960s.

****

Two major differences in 1960 was the walking

mailman, who carried a huge pack on his back and the paperboy who threw papers from his bike basket or a pack on his back like the mailman. Where we lived in Norfolk, Virginia, there was a morning paper and an afternoon paper. Typically, though, a family would only get one or the other. The paperboy also collected the money from his route from each family at least every other week. Poor boy when the people didn't pay! The mailman also went to each family's door as all mailboxes were positioned on the house by the front door, and he – probably never a she – carried his pack, and walked up to the front stoop to put the mail in the box. If a letter was to be picked up and mailed, it was hung on the mailbox with a clothes pin, and the mailman picked it up when he delivered the mail. (Just thinking about it – everything was quite simple during that time).

There were free-standing blue mailboxes (those that are still located outside post offices and a few around some cities today) positioned on many corners of the city, and the mail was picked up there daily by the postman – when he wasn't walking and delivering mail. I believe the job may have been quite difficult for the postman in the 1960s, but being able to drop a letter in the mailbox on the corner if one were running errands sure made it easier than going all the way to the post office.

There were no zip codes at that time, but there were zone numbers, indicating to the post office in which location the mail was to be delivered. On an envelope the zone number was located in the middle of the city and state; such as, Norfolk 3, Virginia. Nevertheless, zip codes ultimately replaced zone numbers. It took a while for those of us to get used to eliminating zone numbers and adding zip codes. When I wrote my friends in another state, I always used the zone number and zip code. I remember Paula's dad telling me that was quite unnecessary when I had said I used both of the numbers when mailing letters. Eventually I learned the proper way.

Like mailboxes that are no longer found on the sides of roads at many corners in 2016, neither are telephone booths. In the 1960s, they were plentiful and found in various parts of a city. The ultimate phone booth was taller than the six foot man, was glass all around, had a folding door that closed, a seat, a phone, and a phone book. Long distance as well as local calls could be made – at a price! Generally, it was only ten cents for a local call but quite a bit more for a long distance call. The price depended on how far the long distance was from the person calling. If someone lived in New York and wanted to call California, it was higher than if someone lived in Tennessee and wanted to call Alabama. To make a long distance call, an operator made the connection – a person! No automation in 1960. The caller told the operator the number, and she told the caller how much money to deposit, which was usually done in quarters, dimes, and nickels. The call generally lasted for three minutes, then the operator would come on the line to tell the caller to end the call or insert more money. If the call was not ended and no money was inserted, the operator ended the call and the line was "dead."

A caller could also place a collect call – only through the operator. When doing so, the caller gave the operator the number to be called as well as his/her name. She, then, would call the number and ask the person answering if he/she would accept a collect call from the caller. If the person said "yes," the call began – at the expense of the person answering. If the person said "no," the call was ended. Nothing was said between the caller and the person answering.

There were no cell phones or texting, but there were expensive long distance calls. People hated to make those collect calls if it weren't necessary, so there were other "ways" of getting a message to a recipient. If one traveled and wanted a person to know he/she had arrived safely, that person made a collect call using a designated name. When the recipient heard that name given by the operator, the answer would be "no" not to accept the collect call. The recipient knew the person had arrived at the destination safely, and no money was spent on a long distance call.

Though there was little if no automation during the 1960s, it was making its debut slowly. I can remember riding in elevators that were the new innovation of automation – I had to push the button for the floor I wanted all by myself! Generally, there had been a person that would open and close the elevator doors as well as push the correct button for the chosen floor. Buttons may not have actually been used before automation, but perhaps another type of contraption was used instead.

The disappearance of the mailboxes and telephone booths are reminiscent of our time when people shop any day of the week, twenty-four hours a day. In 1960, stores were not open on Sunday unless it was a specific drugstore so people could buy medical items. The stores also closed early in the evening, and then opened back up the next morning. There were no supermarkets, malls, few fast food places, and certainly nothing that stayed open all night. As mentioned before, supermarkets were generally a mom and pop store or a small chain located in a certain city, with prices on each individual item that was purchased. The item was rung up by one person with his/her hand calculating everything on a cash register – no bar codes existed.

Shopping areas were not malls but were located in the downtown area of the city or in areas in the city that had a string of a few stores together, but nothing like the double decker malls we have in 2016.

The five and dime stores also existed then – Kresge's, McCrory's, Ben Franklin, Woolworth's and others. Everything was much cheaper at these stores than the bigger stores (the ones strung together in an area) or the downtown stores. To be sure, though, just about anything one needed could be found in the five and dime stores, including food. The lunch counter with bar stools allowed the "lunch crowd" to satisfy a hunger need. Also the name "soda jerks" would have been coined then because they pulled a handle from a big drink container to fill a glass for sodas. For the greater shopping, though, the downtown stores were the big treat, many times with the entire family. Of course, lest anyone forget, one generally dressed up to do so.

Fast food places would have been a novelty in 1960, and I can remember only one that existed. Few people – especially my father – did not want to pay the fifty cents it cost to buy a hamburger at a fast food place. At that time, dinner at home as a family was still the norm; few people ate on the run as they do today in 2016.

Gas for the cars was quite inexpensive at

twenty-five cents per gallon. When there were price wars – lasting usually a day or so -- the price would drop to about fifteen cents per gallon. Also gassing up at a filling station was a luxury compared to 2016. The attendant came to the driver's car window, asked how much gas the driver wanted, pumped the gas, washed the car windows, asked to check the oil and tires, then took the driver's cash – no credit cards would have been seen – and brought back the change.

    Many cars were bigger in the 1960s than what is seen in 2016. According to Jon, many had big fins and hood ornaments! Also, some had seat belts, but a good many did not even have them. When the seat belts were in the cars, they were like the ones seen on airplanes – they just buckled at the waist and never around the shoulder too. There were also no car seats for babies or children. The children were held in the parents' lap, situated between the parents in the front seat, or they sat or stood on the back seat. Some like Jon "rode under the back window when I was small." Speed was obviously reduced, though, as the interstates were just making their debut. Riding down what we would call the backroads today were a cause for slower speeds. Therefore, too, no road rage!

Preparation for air travel was totally different in that era of long ago. Tickets for flights had to be purchased either by calling the specific airline or going to the airport and getting them. Whichever the case, the tickets had to be in hand by the time the traveler needed to board the airplane. Boarding was totally different because the traveler carried – no wheels on luggage – his or her suitcases to the plane once the ticket was taken by the boarding agent. At the airplane, everyone stood with their luggage while it was put inside the plane's baggage compartment. Once the suitcases were stowed away in the airplane, everyone was ready to board. Metal stair steps were wheeled to the airplane door, and everyone walked up the steps and into the plane.

Airline seats were assigned like they are on many airplanes today, and there were also smoking and non-smoking areas in the plane. The choice was made when purchasing the ticket. Food was also served – not a full meal, but a type of food service (sandwiches, etc.) -- more so than the packages of peanuts we receive today on the airplanes. Lastly, pleasing to the eye were the stewardesses, who wore dresses/skirts and jackets as well as heels. Some also wore little hats that depicted the specific airline.

In all instances, from telephones, to gas attendants, to the mailman, to the paperboy, people interacted with people and there was little, or none at all, automation. While some automation is nice, we considered it much nicer to have the voice on the other end of the phone or person outside by the car or the mailman coming up to the doorstep to deliver the mail. It was a time of people, friendship, and caring – it was a time for the good side of memory.

Extra Thoughts:

Linoleum floors

Gold/green appliances

Red and white checkered plastic table cloths

Gold carpet

Wall-to-wall carpeting

Wallpaper

Telephone wires and electrical wires were strung from poles to roof tops

Awnings over windows and doors

Porch swings

Neighborhood kids playing Monopoly on front porches

Unlocked doors

Early bedtime

Family reunions at parks or homes

No air conditioner in cars

No bucket seats in cars

Ash trays in cars

Aluminum Christmas trees with colored wheel light

Bomb scares – students hid under desks when

loudspeakers gave the command
Rulers smacked hands for slight misbehavior
Pregnancies caused students to "disappear"
Bells rang to change classrooms
Student crossing guards
Card catalogue
Due date stamped on book card to return to library

II

Neighbors and Home: Television and Music

Was our house perfect like I thought? No, of course not. Were our neighbors? They may not have been, but I thought they were – most of them anyway. Paula remembers the neighborhood as "Living in a small town or community where everyone knew everyone. The neighbors were all unique and interesting in their own way. It was as if we lived in our own little bubble."

Paula and I also remembered two of our more unique, colorful neighbors – the sexual pervert and the local drunk. The two of us tried to stay out of their way any time we saw them, especially the sexual pervert, who was older – a grandfather – which seemed to us that much more disgusting. A short man, generally clad in jeans and a work shirt, sporting a stubble of a beard, and one who we always said gave us goosebumps. He lived directly across the street from my family and beside the local drunk. He liked to touch little girls inappropriately, and at the age of ten and eleven years, we knew we didn't like what he tried to do; however, we didn't know then that it was sexual perversion. We talked about it ourselves, but we never told our parents – although we should have. Generally, when we saw him crossing the street from his house to our house, we scooted indoors. We were then safe!!

Other people like David, who lived two streets over from our house, had his own unique and colorful neighbors, "The majority consisted of blue collar, solid citizens, but we did have a family of bad eggs whose two sons ended up in jail and/or getting killed in knife or gunfights once they left home." Or like Carol Cole of Tennessee who had her own variety of colorful neighbors: "One lady, renamed The Talking Mule by my dad, kept her carpets covered in plastic lest a speck of dirt defile them. She had a sixth sense about when I was likely to be playing near her precious row of lawn ornaments in her front yard. Another neighbor was an alcoholic gun collector and thus disqualified as a suitable host for neighborhood kids playing in his yard. And lastly, the mean neighbor with the mouth in need of a bar of soap. Everyone shunned him after he deliberately peed on our newly constructed fort of stacked maple leaves."

Some like Brenda Fye of Indiana and Kim Matthews of New Jersey enjoyed having their grandparents live with them rather than be near them as neighbors. It was a time when older parents – grandparents – lived with the family. No one thought anything differently – it was just something that was done, and everyone enjoyed it. Years later, my own grandmother took turns living with her children – my dad being one of her sons. Every three months, she would move out and move in with another child. Since there were eight children, she had plenty of places to go and enjoyed spending time with everyone in her last days.

We really knew our neighbors in the 1960s – they were more than just acquaintances -- and often times, we sat together in the front yard in lawn chairs talking as the sun set and darkness enveloped us. Many times the kids sat with their parents, or they chose to scurry to their own place so they could talk "in private." Neighbors were friendly people and hard-working people. After a day at work, a good supper, we found ourselves in those lawn chairs outside because visiting seemed the perfect way to end the day.

Mary Lou Graham of Tennessee thought, as I did, that her neighbors were friendly, although hers were elderly neighbors. As I think back on it, the neighbors to our right were older as were the ones in the two houses across the street. Paula and her family lived cater-corner to us; however, her parents, the Rapisardis, were not elderly. Mr. Rapisardi, worked hard and Mrs. Rapisardi was a stay-at-home mom, like many of the moms during that era. My own mother stayed home some of the time, and other times, she worked off and on as a librarian. Incidentally, there was no daycare in that era, which made a huge difference in whether Mom went to work or not

Before the boy next door, Bubba Williams, moved in, the previous neighbors living in his house were also elderly. Subsequently, the husband died, and the wife moved away to go stay with her sister. The house remained empty until Bubba and his family moved in. When that happened, it seemed youth was more prevalent than the elderly in our neighborhood, and the young came from down the road and streets away to visit and "hang out" on our street. It was then rockin' on Lenox Avenue. Lenox Avenue – I smile!

Rockin is actually what one would call it in 2016 as a scurry of activity happens every day from the beginning of the day until it ends with parents and children alike falling into bed exhausted. It is a time when both parents work, everyone is up early, breakfast – if eaten – is eaten on the run, kids are dispersed, parents speed to work (not really speeding against the law, but just traveling fast – 75 mph – down the interstate), come back home in the evening, pick up something to eat for supper on the way, do housework (and homework if the kids are older), then fall into bed completely exhausted. The next day, it all starts again!

The scenario, in comparison, was quite different in the 1960s. The day would have been totally altered since, as I mentioned, a good many moms did not work outside of the home. Consequently, getting up was later, unhurried with the exception of getting Dad off to work and older the kids out the door for school. Breakfast would have been more than a breakfast bar as in 2016 – which no one had at that time – but would have been something prepared by Mom. Everyone ate heartily before school and before Dad went to work. No one thought of speeding to work since the interstates were becoming a thought and were on the horizon, but not yet completed. Mom would have cleaned the house, took care of the younger kids, perhaps visited with other neighbors who also were home with younger children. Once the older kids came home from school, they would have had chores to do or homework to complete. Once Dad came back home, everyone would sit down to a home-cooked meal. There was time, then, to enjoy each other and the neighbors outside.

While everyone in our area sat in the front yard talking over the day's events, Lynn and their neighbors sat on the porches, speaking to all passing by. In her neighborhood, everyone kept watch on everyone else, and doors were never locked except when neighbors went out of town. Dianne G. of

Tennessee agreed. No one said the words, "I don't want to get involved." Everyone was involved – not being nosy, but being good, caring neighbors. Dianne said that after fifty years, she is still friends with some of those same neighbors.

Neighbors walked to each other's houses to visit – an invitation was not needed – drop-ins were prevalent. Chris Hoffman of California said one of his neighbors, a hunter and athletic man, came to his house to play ping pong with him on any one given evening. And on many occasions, Bubba found his way over to Mr. Rapisardi's garage to check out any new wood workings he had built and to simply talk with him. When someone came to the door, it was a welcomed sight, and no one stood on the formality of needing an invitation to come visit.

Unlike Dianne's neighbors, I believe most of the neighbors on Lenox Avenue are no longer living with the exception of the children – Paula, Bubba, Bubba's brother, and me. Paula and I have remained friends over these fifty-five years, and I have just re-connected by telephone with Bubba as well as David after all these years. I so remember fondly each of these neighbors, especially Bubba's Mom, Mrs. Williams, and Paula's mom, Mrs. Rapisardi. Mrs. Williams was a single mom, who worked hard to rear two boys alone. My father always said it was a tribute to her to see the results of how she reared the two boys all on her own. In Bubba's own words, "What a woman and Mother she was." I smile when I think of her and all that she meant to me. I wanted to spend as much time as possible at her house as she was always ready with the advice – good or bad – and I accepted it all exactly as she said. David also found her to be someone special with all the kids, and he used to refer to her as Mom #2. She was easy to talk to, fun to be with, but when she said it was time to go home, she sent us away. I was fortunate enough to see her years later when she had remarried. She was happy within herself, and she was ever so pretty – marrying had certainly agreed with her. She has since passed away, but her legacy through her sons and those of us who knew her, lives on in very special memories.

Mrs. Rapisardi was another mom I enjoyed being around. She was quiet, took care of her family, cooked, and cleaned. I always thought it was amazing that she wore dresses around the house when she cleaned and cooked. She could have been one of the women in a TV commercial or one like June Cleaver on the "Leave It To Beaver" show, who never stepped out of her dress. In addition to her dresses, I thought Mrs. Rapisardi to be a beautiful woman. She had long, jet black hair that she would roll up into a flip, and she had skin that was flawless. It was soft, smooth -- wrinkle free. She told us many times that she attributed it all to Pond's Cold Cream. I also was fortunate to see her throughout her years as she aged; however, I never really saw the aging! She was still a beautiful woman into her 70s. I can remember her saying in her later life, possibly in her early 80s, "I see a gray hair!" She touched her hair, and I had to laugh – still beautiful, still black headed – with one gray hair!

I can't think of Lenox Avenue without thinking of Mrs. Williams and Mrs. Rapisardi, two very special ladies in my life. I spent most of my days at one or the other of their houses unless everyone was at my house. One of our houses at any given time always had kids. None of our parents minded when the kids came, playing, talking, or eating – they embraced it.

As mentioned before, dinner time was spent in most houses with families around a table on a nightly basis, and the time was quite structured at least for two of our houses – mine and Paula's. Mr. Rapisardi would step outside on the porch stoop of their house and whistle once – loudly – for Paula to come home at 5:30. It was time for her to come eat, and regardless of what she was doing, she dropped everything to go home when she heard the whistle. But, at 6:00 when it was time for me to eat dinner, Paula, already having eaten at her house, came back over to see what we were having to eat. Many nights she ate her second dinner at our house.

Seldom did we eat dinner with other families, but one of my favorite memories is my parents and I going to the Williams' house where we made homemade snow ice cream – after dinner dessert. Someone had a crank ice cream maker and after gathering plenty of snow, the rock salt, and whatever else that went into the maker, we took turns cranking and waiting for the snow ice cream to harden. When it was finally ready, we ate as if we hadn't eaten before. It was absolutely delicious, and there wasn't a bit left. I don't know that we made anymore again, but that memory has always been vivid to me. It wasn't just the good tasting ice cream, but the gathering together of friends, laughing, and just enjoying each other's company over something as simple as a crank ice cream maker.

Neighbors to our left, as I mentioned, were elderly and really dear people. We kids called the husband "Eagle Eye" because he would walk up and down our sidewalk with his hands behind his back, watching everything we were doing. If he thought something was not proper, he would inform our parents. It wasn't that he was "tattling" but he thought he was doing what was right in making sure we were behaving. Like Bubba said, "He could tell you every little thing that went on within our block, but what a great neighbor he was." Truly, neighbors cared, and they took care of each other – and the children. The parents also accepted what the neighbor might say. No one became upset, no one countered with anger. It was just acceptable!

The Good Side of Memory

****

After dinner and after the dishes had been washed – by hand -- it would be a quiet night with the family, either outside with the neighbors or inside together in the living room, sitting before the television set. The entire family – parents and children – sat before the television set in the living room because most families had only one television. A night would be entertaining with favorite shows and, like at Paula's house, with bowls of popcorn as an enhancement. My family seldom ate anything, unless it was the occasional bowl of ice cream; we just watched the TV.

The 1960s television set was completely unlike what is seen in 2016, which could be a possible sixty-inch wall hanging unit. The set of long ago was small, about ten inches square or round, had two knobs under the picture screen – one for volume and one for changing the channels. By changing the channels, one had to actually get off the couch – usually one of the kids – and turn the knob to the proper channel. No remotes existed in the 1960s. While in 2016, there are hundreds of channels; in

1960, there weren't a variety of channels from which to choose – just the main three: ABC, NBC, and CBS. Perhaps an educational channel, but our family didn't have one.

Some television sets were fancy and sat within a console, but we had a free standing television set on four legs. Nothing fancy about it! It was specifically for entertainment and not beauty. Of course, the "rabbit ears" graced every television on its top. These were a type of antennae and every person had the type they preferred. The "ears" were moved forward, backward, or side to side to find the best reception. Bad weather? Forget good reception! Typically, one could also see the occasional aluminum foil wrapped around the antennae for better reception. Again, nothing fancy about that!

Fancy might be a word to describe the 2016 flat screen TV that, as mentioned, can be placed on the wall. In 1960, it would have been impossible to put the TV on the wall since it was big and bulky with tubes and all kinds of electrical paraphernalia located in the back of it. Tubes had to be changed, other little electrical things had to be changed, and if the picture tube itself went out, it probably would have been better to purchase a new television set!

Television shows were in black and white at the start of the 1960s. But by the end of the decade, color was making its appearance; nevertheless, it came at a price. My father was adamant, though – "No need to pay extra for color. We can see everything just fine in black and white!" I would be remiss if I didn't admit that I probably was a typical teen even back then that said, "But everybody is getting color." Not a go for my dad – he didn't buy into that fallacy. I sighed and continued watching the TV in black and white. By the time I left their home as a young adult, though, he was just beginning to think that color may not be so bad after all!

At our house, my choice was not a concern of what to watch on the television but solely that of my dad's. Consequently, we watched what he wanted to watch and if I didn't like what we were watching, I had to find something else to do. Quietly! No talking, hollering, or fussing when my dad was watching his show! Readers might think there would be plenty to do in my room if I didn't want to watch television, but – remember -- there were no computers, no videos, no CDs, no cell phones, and certainly not another television set. I could read a book or a magazine, listen to the radio, or play my records. Whatever I chose to do, I would do it quietly.

While I could only watch what my dad desired to watch, Jan was only allowed certain shows each week. "Our family acquired a television set while I was still young. However, we were only allowed to watch a few pre-selected shows per week. My parents were convinced that reading library books, being outdoors, and playing imaginatively were better for us than TV!"

There was no twenty-four/seven television viewing time in 1960. At the end of the news, for us on eastern time, it was 11:00 p.m. (I had long been in bed, so that didn't pertain to me), the television stations signed off. Someone announced the signing off, a little music played, a black and white round symbol showed on the screen, and then the television screen was blank. It would resume sometime in the morning hours.

While the television was turned on over the

course of the day and evening, there were a good variety of shows from action, drama, comedy, variety and others from which to choose. In our house, westerns dominated because my dad loved them. I did like a few of them as did many others. One that I especially liked as did Kathy Schlegel of Pennsylvania and Elaine Rose of Oregon, was "Bonanza." I believe all of the young girls were in love with Little Joe, the youngest of those Cartwright boys! Another favorite western was "Gunsmoke" especially for Brenda since her grandmother had the thrill of talking to Matt Dillon (James Arness in real life) in person.

With the westerns, there was "shoot'em up bang bang" but no blood, nothing gruesome, just victims falling to the ground dead. And sex? Absolutely not shown. In "Gunsmoke" when Matt Dillon went up the saloon stairs to the next floor with Miss Kitty, you knew what was happening, but it was never shown.

Comedy was also a favorite of the television shows in the 1960s and the one dominating for everyone was "I Love Lucy." It was simple, a slap stick type, and funny. Like our own families, the two couples in the show (Ricardos and Mertzes) represented a good many of the households of the time. The women stayed home, men worked; women wore dresses – even to clean the house – make-up and hair was always fixed; and when the cameras allowed, there were always twin beds in the bedroom! All quite unlike our comedy shows of 2016; specifically, sex was never mentioned, most of the body was covered, and a light peck on the cheek sufficed for a kiss. Other popular comedies: "The Honeymooners," "Andy Griffith," "My Three Sons," "The Addams Family," "Bewitched," "Leave It To Beaver," and "The Beverly Hillbillies." Even adult cartoons took over prime time with "The Flintstones." Of course the kids liked it too, and at any given time of the day, people could be heard saying, "Yabba, dabba, do!"

Other phrases bring specific shows to mind, and I challenge you readers to remember these: "Just the facts, ma'am. Just the facts," "You have entered another dimension, another time," "It's a plane, it's a bird, it's….," "To the moon, Alice, to the moon," "Keep them doggies rollin'….," "A horse is a horse, of course, of course," "Ahhh, mon chiere," "Nip it in the bud," "Would you believe..." "Danger, Danger, Will Robinson," "And that's the way it is," "Now cut that out," "We've got a really big show," "Work!" "Hi-Oh Silver!" "You rang?"

Variety shows also dominated the air waves such as "The Ed Sullivan" show, which was the most popular. Young kids found themselves watching old Ed Sullivan because he was the first to have rock n roll singers such as Elvis, The Beatles, and so many others on his show. While I sat on the floor and was mesmerized by the rock n roll stars that filed through the Ed Sullivan Sunday night show, my parents grimaced each time they came on. They were definitely not fans of rock n roll! They favored the quieter country music where the performers didn't move around as much and "didn't scream the lyrics" as my dad often said. Brenda was a fan of the "Jack Benny Show", Fred and I favored "The Walt Disney Show", and my parents and I also liked "The Loretta Young Show." When Donna and her family bought their first color TV, they were ecstatic. "It was placed in its 'honored' spot in the living room. Wow -- color on Sunday night when Disney's "Wonderful Word of

Color" came on and Tinkerbell used her wand to magically create color on that screen, our eyes lit up! Everyone had beaming smiles on their faces! Of course, Dad was partial to the map that went up in flames when "Bonanza" came on! Those Cartwright boys were something else!"

Medical shows were also a favorite, such as, "Dr. Kildare" and "Ben Casey." Carolyn Martin of Japan was able to watch and hear "Ben Casey" through the sound on Armed Forces radio. By turning off the television sound and listening to the radio, she and her family were able to watch their favorite show on the television and listen to it in English on the radio. Because the show was the family favorite, the night it was watched (and heard) was Carolyn's only night she could stay up late on a school night!

Some shows the younger ones enjoyed, such as Fred and Jon, were "Lassie," "Roy Rogers," "The Lone Ranger," and "Hop a Long Cassidy." Others enjoyed "Mighty Mouse," "Woody Woodpecker," and "Bugs Bunny." Of course, cartoons dominated the morning hours as did "Captain Kangaroo." And who of us could forget the Mickey Mouse Club –

Annette Funicello – and Mr. Green Jeans, the friend of the Captain.

The all time favorite for every teen, of course, was "American Bandstand," which lasted over the course of two decades, with Dick Clark being the forever teen-ager! We watched every afternoon, we knew the regular dancers on the show, and we tried to imitate every new dance that came on the show. A new singer or one that was already established generally performed on "American Bandstand" every time it was on. Therefore, it was also another time teens could see their favorite rock n roll stars other than on "The Ed Sullivan Show."

Space also entered the television hour with "Star Trek," "My Favorite Martian" and "Lost in Space." For those that liked the steamy side – no kids allowed -- it was "Peyton Place."

****

For adults and kids alike, music dominated the era. While most kids certainly favored rock n roll, my parents, and a good many others, couldn't get enough of country music. Consequently, I really didn't like country music since I had to listen to it at home if I were downstairs with my parents as well as listen to it while riding in the car with them. Although, I have to admit, I do know the lyrics to songs by Hank Williams, Tennessee Ernie Ford, Jim Reeves, and more. And many times, I found myself singing "Your Cheatin' Heart" with my mother as we cleaned house.

Nevertheless, often I gravitated to my room so I could listen to my own music. Music that was played on a little record player which had to have the record put on manually to be played each time. Most of these records were the little 45s. I didn't really get my first 33 1/3 LP album until the age of twelve on one Christmas morning – one that I will never forget. All presents had been opened, and I was quite disappointed because I had been asking for an album by none other than my favorite singer – Elvis Presley. My dad had hidden the album behind the couch, and during my smiling/sulking period, he told me to check out something behind the couch. I thought that quite odd, and when I looked, I found the "Rip It Up" album by Elvis. I played it all day on my little record player and couldn't have been happier. That very album was my first and it, along with about thirty other Elvis albums as well as many others, still adorn my storage room! I wouldn't dream of parting with any of them.

While we kids listened to our favorite singers, the only time we really were able to see them and see what they looked like was in magazines. Since there were no computers, there was no YouTube, certainly no MTV, it was either magazines or on one of the variety shows that we could lay eyes on our favorite rocker. We heard our favorite singers through records, and we may have seen them on "The Ed Sullivan Show" or "American Bandstand," but we really didn't know much about them except through the coveted magazines that featured the singers and a story or two about them. Of course Elvis, my favorite as well as the favorite of many young girls, had played in numerous movies, something the other singers had not done yet. His were movies about singing with a silly plot that had many girls running around everywhere, usually pining after him in some fashion! I write now that they were silly, but I didn't think so, nor did the other young girls, when I went to the theater to see them in my young years. My favorite

Elvis movie was "Blue Hawaii," but one of his first, "Love Me Tender" captured the hearts of many, and we shed tears at the end when Elvis died.

We watched movies, sought out magazines, and searched for any 8 x 10 pictures we could get through the fan clubs of our favorite singers. Anything to look at them and see what we generally had only previously heard on the radio! Even record album covers and the 45 single jackets were also coveted since they would carry a picture or two on them.

It would seem that Elvis was one of the first artists, if not THE artist, to really break into rock n roll and become the sensation he was known for during his short life. Girls swooned over his songs like "Love Me Tender" and "Treat Me Nice," and took in every movement allowed on "The Ed Sullivan Show." But those sightings of his movements were few since he was only allowed to be filmed from the waist up. He was considered far too racy from the waist down, acquiring the name "Elvis the Pelvis." Parents really didn't want their kids watching him nor even listening to his music. Nevertheless, that seemed to fall on deaf ears since the sensation of Elvis was everywhere, and every kid wanted to listen to him. Parents acquiesced.

A tamer sort – ones with less movements -- were those sought out by Mary Lou and Lynn; specifically, Johnny Mathis, Ricky Nelson, and Gene Pitney. Groups also became popular quickly such as The Platters, The Temptations, and The Association. A favorite group for Donna, whom she saw in concert, was The Monkees. The biggest group sensation, though, according to Larry Velasquez of Florida and Brenda were the Beach Boys. Kids loved that beach music from surfing to cars to those special California girls.

Another sensation to burst on the scene was Chubby Checker and his rendition of the new dance craze, the Twist. Gone was the jitterbug that highlighted American Bandstand – now it was the Twist, seen all over the states in every dance venue. Even my parents thought it was amazing that everyone was doing this crazy dance and when their friends came to the house to socialize, they all wanted Paula and I to do the Twist and "perform" for them. We were quite accommodating and quite willing to do our favorite dance for them.

Women singers were just as popular as the male singers with Brenda Lee, Leslie Gore, and Carol King topping the charts. Of course it would seem Diana Ross and the Supremes were the main head liners, and Ms. Ross would continue her career in decades to follow, although she would do it alone. In the years to come, she was no longer a part of the Supremes.

Kathy Schlegel, Bubba, and Lali also liked Motown; in fact, Kathy said, "It was Motown all the way. I guess we were so close to Philadelphia that it stuck. Love it all!" So, The Temptations were quite popular with their number one hit song, "My Girl," one that Bubba favored and one that everyone went around singing.

David liked something a little different than what a good many of the tweens and teens were listening to in the 1960s. While he favored the Beatles, Elvis, and Jerry Lee Lewis, he also liked classical music such as that associated with Peter and the Wolf. "I also liked some of the older popular music my folks liked – songs by Sinatra, Crosby, Andy Williams, Nat King Cole, just to name a few."

If the parents thought it was "different" with Elvis, they were appalled when The Beatles came on the scene with the first of the long hair on boys. They were seen not only on "The Ed Sullivan Show" but also on the nightly news when their plane landed in America from Liverpool. These four young British men stepped out on the tarmac to girls screaming, crying, and fainting. Girls pulled their hair, shouted the name of their favorite Beatle, and tried to break through the police line, who tried to keep them back. It had all not been seen in any manner like that before, and Beatlemania was definitely the next sensation.

Now it wasn't Elvis, Chubby Checker, or Ricky Nelson that took rock n roll to the new level, but it was the Beatles. By the end of the 1960s, the hair sported by the Beatles that barely touched their ears when they came to America in 1964 now hovered around boys' shoulders and sometimes longer. The music had taken on an entirely new fashion with lyrics that screamed war and drugs. The Twist was left far behind, and the dirty dog graced the dance floors. If parents thought the gyrations of Elvis were bad, they cringed at the dance moves of the dirty dog.

In a gentler time, though, before the hippie movement, heavy metal, and the sexual revolution brought the 1960s to a close, the early 1960s were still rife with playing records, listening to the transistor radio, and enjoying music with simple lyrics. These easy songs were what we heard played every night as the Top Ten favorite songs on radio stations probably in every teen's bedroom. I preferred – WGH radio. Same time, same station, same DJ! Others listened to different stations and different DJs in Norfolk, but the Top Ten was still played nightly by most of them. Great songs were played, and I, as well as all my friends, had our ears tuned in to the Top Ten each night. These were the songs that held the spot in the beginning of the 60s for a long period of time: The Twist, Stuck on You, It's Now or Never, Handy Man, I'm Sorry, Teen Angel, Running Bear, Cathy's Clown, He'll Have to Go, and Theme From a Summer Place.

Chris and his brother also listened to their own stations' top ten hits in California as well as the afternoon call-in requests and dedications. Like many, he favored the Beach Boys and Jan and Dean because of his California ties.

Records were inexpensive at the time; well, probably part of a week's allowance – they were ninety-nine cents. We purchased the ones we had heard from the Top Ten, brought them home, and played them over and over on our record players. While listening, we would scour those magazines looking for pictures of our favorite singer and try to envision what he/she looked like while the music played in the background. We would envision, would sway to the music, and would clutch the picture to our chests (perhaps this was just a girl thing). Yes, it was a different time, one that I look back on and simply smile.

Extra Thoughts:

Have Gun Will Travel

Make Room for Daddy

Rawhide

Sugarfoot

Broken Arrow

The Adventures of Ozzie and Harriet

The Real McCoys

77 Sunset Strip

The Red Skelton Show

Many Lives of Dobie Gillis

McHale's Navy

Hazel

Petticoat Junction

Get Smart

Rocky and Bullwinkle

Lost in Space

Gilligan's Island

Batman

Superman

Popeye

The Good Side of Memory

Heckle and Jeckle

Tom and Jerry

Huntley/Brinkley Hour

Walter Cronkite

Jackie Wilson

The Shirelles

The Ronettes

Righteous Brothers

Mamas and the Papas

Sonny and Cher

Paul Harvey and the rest of the story

Mitch Miller

"Are You Lonesome Tonight?"

"A Hard Day's Night"

"It's My Party"

"Roses Are Red"

"Da Doo Ron Ron"

First Super Bowl

Hippies

Woodstock

III

Parents, Children, Eating Out

Most parents and children were involved as a family in the 1960s; however, David summed up Mom and Dad quite nicely. "They were honest folk who stressed the importance of character, hard work, and common sense. Mom was very religious for someone who did not attend church, which, as a child and young adult, had been her second home where she grew up in New York. She was a gentle, angel of a mom but she could be very firm as well. Dad was a bull in a china shop when it came to opinions. He had a deep, commanding voice, and he spent many hours with me as a kid teaching me how to work and play hard. Fair play was a must and was far more important than winning. He also taught me how to stay strong and fit."

In 2016, parents and children see little of each other, sometimes not at all in the course of the day. Working parents, day care, school activities, sports, dinner on the run, and working teens seem to keep parents and children apart. Dad may get home late or Mom may have a moment to pick up the children only to drop them in front of the television so she can have some time alone – or time to take care of the house.

Fifty years ago, there were few working moms, although some did work outside of the home. There was no day care, and school activities were kept at a minimum and completed before dinner time, which was a family affair. An affair that gave parents and children time to talk, time to say what they had on their minds, and just a time for enjoyment. Of course, not that all dinner time was perfect – kids still didn't like what mom put on their plates and kids still refused to eat, but most of the time, it went off "without a hitch" as my dad often said.

Dinners, themselves, may have been different in the 1960s in that a few certain meals were eaten over and over. In 2016, I have hundreds of cook books and love to try something new every day; however, Fred's mother cooked certain dinners on certain nights of the week, and always a pot roast on Sundays. Kathy Steenson of Florida said her mom cooked continually and baked cakes and pies daily. "Any leftovers would be the main ingredient of breakfast the following morning. When my siblings and I returned home from school each afternoon, we were welcomed by the scent of freshly baked cookies."

Like me, many kids were involved with their parents. Dianne's mother was the room mother at her school, the scout leader, and, together, her family went boating, swimming, fishing, and skiing. My mother was also a room mother at my school – until Junior High, when having room mothers stopped. At any given time, though, she helped in the elementary classroom, brought food, taught the hula (one of our many moves was to Hawaii) to the girls in the classroom, and so much more. And every child knew that my mother made the best cream puffs! Any time there was a party – and they were plentiful – they always asked for the cream puffs. It was my mother's "claim to fame."

Donna and her family sang while her dad and uncles played their guitars. "My fondest memories were of family gatherings and them playing music and all of us kids sitting in the floor and singing along. 'B-I-N-G-O,' 'She'll be Coming Around the Mountain,' 'Oh, Suzannah,' etc… Ahhh, those are wonderful memories. We laughed so hard we cried."

Brenda was an only child and very close to her family especially when the weekend arrived. "Because my mother did not drive, my parents and I, and my grandmother as well while she lived with us, would go to a larger neighboring town every Saturday to shop and buy groceries. We would eat out for lunch there before going to the grocery stores." It was a fun day for the entire family.

Kathy Steenson and her family had a boat that they kept tied up in the canal behind their house. Her dad took the family skiing often, especially on Christmas Day. Whether it was "being a girl" or not, her dad couldn't teach her to ski. "For some reason, Dad could never teach me to ski, but I loved to ride fast in the boat while my brothers skied."

While Dianne and her family and Kathy and her family were the outdoorsy type, mine were the inside type. My mother and I, like Kathy Schlegel and Kathy Steenson and their moms, played cards and board games such as Scrabble and Monopoly. Mother's card games started out simple with Go Fish when she began teaching me, but then she taught me Rummy, my card playing was never the same. In fact, my card playing days were "legendary;" specifically with my dad, who was quite competitive when it came to cards or, actually, any type of sports. As one might suspect, I inherited those genes! When I began playing cards with my dad, it was in a competitive fashion; when I began bowling with him, we seemed to compete against each other even though we were on the same team; and in golf, we competed but he always had the edge. I could never beat my dad in golf – though I really tried! My dad and I continued our competitive streak in our numerous games of Rummy through my first year of college when I came home on vacation. We had a running tally that we kept day after day until I went back to school. While at home, the house echoed with the call out of "Rummy!" when the cards were slammed to the table – like I said, very competitive!

Incidentally, from bowling to golf to cards, when my dad and I were in competition with each other, neither would give in to the other. I knew when I won a game, I earned it and vice versa with him. We bowled together in leagues and in tournaments, and he had to doff his hat to me when my average exceeded 175 and his stayed at 160. Ahhh, my greatest moment!! Or when he had held on to the high score of 266 for years, until I came in his house one evening with an announcement:

"Guess what I bowled last night?"

Looking at me in a rather suspect fashion, he said, "Can't imagine, but by your look, it must've been good."

"What was your top score," I asked

Now he really became uncertain, took his pipe out of his mouth, and said, "A 266." Narrowing eyes now, "Why do you ask?"

I smiled, "I just bowled a 267."

He only grinned, put his pipe back in his mouth, and nodded in my direction – job well done!

As competitive as my dad and I were, my mother and I were just the opposite. She had taught me how to play cards, but she also taught me to knit and crochet. Together we made house shoes, sweaters, dresses, blankets, and so much more. Likewise, the indoorsy and domesticated type, Lynn learned sewing from her mother; however, I doff my hat to her because I could never make that talent work! Donna, like Lynn and unlike me, loved to sew since she had been in sixth grade. "Mom bought me a kid size Singer sewing machine (manual/hand turning mechanism) that clamped onto a table. I sewed many, many doll clothes out of scrap material." Yes, it was a time when moms and daughters "played" together and daughters learned from mothers.

Shopping was typically done with our parents, and the highlight was to go downtown, and, as I mentioned previously, dressed to the nines to do so. Everyone dressed up to go downtown, some moms even in high heeled shoes. Of course, when heels were worn, hose were worn with them -- the kind with seams up the back of the leg. I couldn't wait until I was old enough so I could wear hose with seams up the back of my leg. Unfortunately, as I became of age to do so, the seams were on the way out of style, and just plain hose were in. Incidentally, the hose were always two separate pieces – like a pair of knee socks – and women wore them with garter belts, which clasped the tops of each hose and held them up mid thigh. I couldn't wait for seams, but I hated the garter belt. Toward the end of the 1960s, panty hose came on the market, and everyone, especially me, loved wearing them. Surprisingly, separate hose are still around, so I assume people still wear garter belts. None of that would be found in my wardrobe! Nevertheless, my oldest and youngest daughters recently told me they both find garter belts sexy. One of my middle daughters hasn't said much about garter belts, but she favors Spanx, and my other middle daughter says "none of that for her!"

It seemed every time I awaited a fashion that I loved on my mother, it went out of style by the time I became old enough to wear it. Specifically, as mentioned, the seam-up-the-leg hose, then the white gloves, and, lastly, the head scarves. With every dress, Mother had a pair of white gloves to wear. I watched her put them on, fixing each finger perfectly. I always thought she looked so lovely with her white gloves and fancy dress. Her head scarves, a beautiful square, thin, silky material were worn anytime she went outside (no messy hair). The square was folded over (corner to corner) into a triangle shape, placed on the head, then tied loosely under the chin. She had many, and, like the gloves, I thought they were beautiful and couldn't wait to have some of my own. Alas, by the time I was a teen-ager, they were out of style and seen no more.

I had somewhat of a say in the clothes and shoes that my parents purchased on our shopping trips, but not as much as I would like. They chose everything for a practical, "long wearing" purpose! Remember the times – durability! My parents certainly adhered to that! Style was not in their repertoire! Specifically, I always had to wear saddle shoes, and I hated them! Other girls would have flats or what they called "trotters." These were worn with no socks or perhaps anklets if they were on the pretty, stylish side. Oh, how I coveted those trotters, and how I hated saddle shoes. With the saddle shoes, it was bobby socks – a much thicker rendition of anklets and always rolled down once or twice – or knee socks. Practical, durable – in my parents' way of thinking; Yuk – in my way of thinking.

As I mentioned before, I was the one washing the dishes with my mother and when we didn't have a maid – we did have one for a while when my mother worked at the library – we also cleaned together. I am sure most children, like me, had specific chores, and those chores had to be done before anything else began. Paula generally had Saturday chores; specifically, cleaning her room. I don't know if she was like me, but what I didn't put away in its proper place was thrown under my bed. I could have had a garage sale (seldom, if ever, saw one of those back then) with everything that was under my bed. Imagine the big surprise of my parents when we moved, and the number of things that were pulled out from under my bed!

Hair was something else that my mother was fanatical about. Perhaps not as much as I grew older, but when I was younger – probably just moving to Lenox Ave and a year or two beyond – I had to have everything out of my eyes or face. Mother was the one who would put my hair in a pony tail, and when she did so, she always told me to grab a chair and hold on! Using a rubber band – no elastic bands or scrunchies existed – she pulled my hair back as tight as she could, and I felt like my eyes were like little slits being pulled back as well. Needless to say, my pony tail stayed in all day, and not a strand of hair came out to get in my face or get in my eyes. When I didn't have long enough hair for a pony tail, she would give me a perm – better known as a permanent then. Not the type of nice perms that we have in 2016. No! In this type of perm, hair was tightly wrapped around little rollers. Pink liquid – poured into a little bowl -- was then squeezed onto each roller with cotton balls. I held a towel to my face so the liquid wouldn't leak onto it, and tried to breathe and not gag from the smell. The liquid odor was horrendous and anyone in 2016 who had a permanent in the 1960s can definitely relate! After a rinsing and the rollers removed, my hair was definitely permed – right to my scalp just about! Oh, how lucky I considered Paula, who had naturally curly hair. Hers was long, pulled gently back into a nice pony tail, and hung in little curls past her shoulders. Mine was curly, too, but like little cork screws sitting close to my head. I could pull a curl away from my head, and it jetsetted straight back into its little cork screw position. My curls were certainly not gentle curls like hers.

Of course, those that had curly hair hated it – as did Paula – and she, as well as others, resorted to ironing their hair to straighten it out. On a real ironing board with a real iron! Unbelievable as that sounds now, it happened with just about everyone with long hair. Curly wanted to be straight – ironing; straight wanted to be curly – permanent!

It seemed the simple look of hair – straight or curly – took on a new look when the massive piled high hair came on the scene. Beehives and bouffants! Girls began teasing or ratting their hair to make it pile up high, then gently combing over the teasing to give it a smoother look. Despite that smooth look, there was quite a bit of teased hair underneath. Combing it all out, once it had been sprayed with hair spray or lacquered with some product that I wasn't familiar with, was a chore within itself. For those of us that didn't succumb to the mile-high hair, we chose page boys or, again, the simple straight or curly look until the likes of Twiggy and Mia Farrow came along with the cute short look cut close to the head. It was quite short and fairly straight – no ironing here, it was too short.

If hair was simply washed and dried, it wasn't dried and brushed with a hand-held dryer as in 2016. No, it had to be rolled with rollers or pin curled with bobby pins, then head and all curled hair put under a plastic-like cap that was attached to the hair dryer with a long tube. This was done if it were a portable hair dryer that many of the households enjoyed. The other kind of hair dryer was a huge metal type that one sat under with the big head part coming over the hair/head. The time was endless, it seemed, and HOT!! I always grabbed a book to pass the time while hair drying. Of course, the dryers were quite loud when drying, and talking to someone was not possible. In order to talk, the hair dryer had to be lifted up, or one poked her head out from under the dryer to listen. Hence, read and wait out the drying time.

It was my mother who showed me the love of reading as she was always with a book in hand – including when she knitted and crocheted. She was able to put the book in her lap, put a clothes pin on each page to hold the book open, and knit or crochet while reading. While I loved to read, I was never that adept at knitting and crocheting without looking at what I was doing – definitely not reading. In our younger years, Mother walked with me to the library (when she wasn't working there herself), and we both picked out books that suited our needs. We would carry arm loads of books from the library, and start reading the minute we returned home. Her love for reading lasted until her final book, with marker in place, that I found on her nightstand.

While it was not prevalent with my family, a good many families took drives on Sundays and visited family and friends. Donna and her family had picnics in the Smokies. "Especially in the fall when the leaves changed colors. Love those memories!" I would have loved to have gone somewhere on Sunday, driving with my parents and eating at a place like Brenda and her family did, or like Donna and her family – a picnic somewhere fun. Nevertheless, eating out was not something my parents ever adhered to – definitely not a picnic – whether it was Sunday or not. My dad always wanted his weekends at home and not driving around in a car. He felt he traveled around enough, whether by car or by ship, while being in the Navy. Taking a nice, quiet Sunday drive was certainly not what he wanted to do. For others, though, visiting and eating out was practically the only activity that took place on Sunday since stores were closed, and no malls existed at that time.

Even though her family wasn't eating out, Jan's Sundays were similar in that the Sabbath was the Sabbath. "We were a church-going family and always had a big dinner after church on Sunday. Mother and Daddy would talk about the day's sermon during dinner while we children ate hurriedly so we could have dessert. The rule: no clean plate no dessert! We could play on Sunday – but we had to play quietly. It was Sunday and we kept the Sabbath."

In 2016, it seems people eat out far more than they eat at home. In 1960, it was simply a rarity for families in many homes. My mother, as were most at that time, was the one "slaving" over the stove. My dad would come home from work, sit down, read the paper, and wait until dinner was ready. The question never came up, "Do you want to go out to eat tonight?" It was assumed my mother, and many mothers like her, would have dinner ready on the table sometime after my dad came home from work.

During that time of the early 60s, fast food restaurants were not the norm as they are today fifty years later. In our town, I only knew of Shoney's Big Boy as a hamburger place – not even called a fast food restaurant. Nevertheless, I believe McDonald's had just appeared on the scene, but I had not had the pleasure of indulging at that eatery! At times some of the kids would ask about going there to get a hamburger, and my dad was adamant with me – "Absolutely not! I'm not paying fifty cents for one hamburger when I can have your mother cook five or six for that same price of a pound of hamburger meat." David's dad essentially said the same thing, "Dad considered restaurants a waste of time and money for food that was not as good as he got at home." And it didn't surprise me when Bubba said, "We seldom went out to eat. My mom was a terrific cook so we ate in a lot, and I miss some of the dishes she used to make. What a cook!"

Because of my dad's stance on eating at

"hamburger joints," I never ate at a fast food restaurant until I was in my later teens, living in Key West, Florida. And I'm sure that I paid for it out of my weekly allowance! Larry said, "We did eat take out at The Hop 4th of July -- good Cuban food sandwiches, black beans, and yellow rice. I do remember the Royal Castle, little square hamburgers. And when they opened the Burger King, everyone from Hey West High would hit that place hard." It was the Burger King at which I ate – with my own allowance – while living in Key West and attending Key West High with Larry.

Mary Lou Graham. only remembered mom and pop restaurants, but she and her family still did not patronize them much except on Sundays if they weren't eating at her grandmother's. Lynn and her family ate out maybe once a year, and Kim said it never happened for her and family – quite a difference than in 2016!

The Good Side of Memory

Extra Thoughts:

Chocolate chip cookies and milk

Cracker Jack toys

Waxed candy lips

Black licorice

JuJu Bees

Yoo Hoo drinks

Bosco

Tang

RC Cola and a Moon Pie

Page boys

Beehives

Duck tails

Pompadour Hairstyle

Sideburns

Madras

Penny loafers

Kilts

Wrap around skirts

Bobbie Brooks clothes

Weejuns

IV

1960s Top News Stories

Today, fifty years after a quiet time in the early 60s, murder, violence, and terrorism seem to be the norm rather than the exception. The kids even play video games spouting these very real crimes and wars as if it is second nature to them. Horrifically, the more gruesome the game, the better! Taking a step back in time, it was games of gruesome murders but games like Concentration, Candy Land, Life, Monopoly, and others that dominated the minds of the young. Obviously, the kids had no video games then, and the closest people came to seeing a murder might have been on a western television show when a gun was fired. There would have been lots of smoke and when it cleared, the target man lay on the ground – no blood around him at all.

Imagine, then, the ghastly news to hit the airwaves that the President of the United States had been shot and later died. The date was November 22, 1963 and while it was not a totally peaceful era, being the time when the black students sit-in at Woolworth's had taken place, the Viet Nam war was going on, and the Cuban Missile Crisis foisted its problems in the media, the news of the presidential shooting was still a complete shock to America and places abroad as well.

I believe every person old enough to know or hear about the news could tell you today exactly where he or she was at that very moment. I sat in 9th grade English class, and our teacher ran into the room crying, she was so overcome with emotion. We students were stunned to see our teacher in tears and unable to speak for a moment. She finally was able to find the words to relay the news that the President had been shot only to hear minutes later when the principal begin speaking over the loudspeaker that President Kennedy had died. No one moved for a period, then our teacher ran out of the room sobbing. As young students, we honestly didn't know what to do, but we did know that this was a terrible, terrible thing to have happened.

Minutes passed and composing herself once more, our teacher came back into the classroom and only said she wouldn't be teaching anything that afternoon, but that we were to read quietly. We did so until the bell rang and everything and everyone erupted in the hallway – shock, disbelief, and alarm were emotions shown on faces and heard in voices. I remember not walking home but literally running home to talk to my parents about this tragic event.

While I was in English class, Kathy Steenson was in gym class. "We were in gym class when the teacher informed us what had happened. The students were told to go to their home rooms, and that was where we stayed until it was time to go home." Lynn said, "I will never forget where I was when the announcement was made. I was in 6th hour biology class my freshman year of high school. It is the only class that I can remember the hour on. I know what classes I took but not when they were." Bubba was on the bus going home from school. "Someone had a transistor radio playing when the news came on about President Kennedy being shot in Dallas, Texas. What a shocker! This was new to me at the time that someone would do such a thing. What a horrific act!"

Almost immediately when the shooting occurred,

television and radio stations were interrupted with the news. From that moment on, and for the next four days, all shows and specific music were suspended. The television stations only carried the up-to-the-minute news about the shooting and the radio stations only played soft music – no rock n roll and no country. By the time I arrived home that day from school, my mother was already sitting in front of the television in a state of shock. When my dad arrived home from work, it was the same for him. He simply kept saying, "This is not supposed to happen in 1963!"

Of course, the shock did not stop with the Kennedy shooting because two days later Lee Harvey Oswald, the alleged suspect of shooting the president, was being transferred to a different venue. People across the globe were literally stunned, as they watched the television, to see a man, Jack Ruby, come out of nowhere, draw a gun, and shoot Oswald. I remember my mother screaming out loud when it happened, and I can imagine people everywhere, in front of their television sets, had that same reaction.

It was a sad time for America and people around

the world as well. Everyone seemed to be affected by this tragic shooting because we thought shootings only took place in westerns (especially in our little bubble of a world) – not in a city known by everyone and not against the President of the United States that was beloved by the masses.

Once the four day suspension was lifted and the television and radio stations resumed their regular broadcasting, everything started getting back to normal. Although normal is really an incorrect word because we were plagued with civil rights marches, which, as I mentioned, included the black students' sit in at the Woolworth's lunch counter. It would seem they were served, but none were too happy about it at the time. We still had separate bathrooms and drinking fountains – coloreds and whites -- but people were beginning to come together. Rosa Parks seemed to have started the movement when she refused to sit in the back of a city bus because she was a colored woman in 1955, but the divide between coloreds and whites was still huge. It would simply take time; more time than people wanted.

While the Kennedy assassination made an impact

on Kathy Steenson, it was the Viet Nam war, which had a lasting impression on her as her family members were fighting there. "My younger brother spent a year there with the Army as a helicopter medic. As the helicopter hovered, he jumped off to bring back bodies and injured personnel. It was one of the most dangerous jobs of the war, so we were extremely fortunate that he returned safe and sound. My future husband spent two years in Viet Nam as a high voltage electrician with the Air Force. He and I wrote daily, fell in love through our letters, got engaged through the mail, he sent my engagement ring in the mail, which I promptly put on myself, and then we married five days after his return from his first Viet Nam tour."

Also headlining the news were protests against the Viet Nam war and issues that had never affected America before were rearing their ugly heads with students, young adults, and older adults as well. We had been through the Cuban Missile Crisis, and, now over seas, the Berlin Wall was being constructed, all of which was dominating the news. Unrest was among us and peace seemed to be a thing of the past.

Mary Lou Graham. remembers the bombings in Birmingham that killed four girls, and Kathy Schlegel could hear gun shots from her front yard during the race riots. Unrest was definitely among us.

Because of his close ties to her community, Brenda said the death of Astronaut Gus Grissom made a huge impact on her life. "He was from my hometown, his parents lived in the next block, and my great grandmother told me we were distantly related to his mother. I remember being at church with the youth group when someone stopped by to let us know about the accident. His funeral was held at the First Baptist Church, and I remember watching out our picture window as the people arrived and all the TV channels set up their cameras."

Before the assassination and while John Kennedy and Richard Nixon battled for the seat of Presidency, the two men had the first live television debate. Though I was young at the time, I do remember the adults talking about these two men during the debate. One quite handsome and seemingly in complete control of himself – John F. Kennedy; the other not quite as handsome and sweating profusely – Richard M. Nixon. The debate was a more stick-to-the-issues event with neither mud-slinging his way through his time slot of talking like we have seen in more recent presidential debates on television in 2016. Kennedy went on from the debate to win the presidential election, and he left quite a legacy in his path. Not only on America herself with the war, crisis abroad, protests, and more, but also with one single sentence that he stated: "Ask not what your country can do for you; ask what you can do for your country."

The Kennedy name and legacy, unfortunately, has been fraught with execrable events since President Kennedy's assassination: the assassination of brother, Robert Kennedy; the questionable debacle of brother, Edward Kennedy and Chappaquidick; son John Kennedy, Jr. dying in a plane crash; nephews dying unexpectedly, and more. Also associated with the Kennedys in the news was Marilyn Monroe's death. Though not associated with the Kennedy name, Martin Luther King was also assassinated in the same year as Robert Kennedy. The peaceful 60s just weren't that peaceful at the end of the decade.

With so much unrest, it wasn't only the national news that was turbulent, but we faced our own ghastly news locally. News that had never happened like it before in our city and especially not on Lenox Avenue. A high school girl was desirous of finding babysitting jobs, and she posted her name, address, and telephone number on the wall at one of the local laundromats. Since there was no social media at the time, putting an ad on a laundromat wall was not that odd. Definitely something that a teen would do in hopes of getting a response.

She did get a response, and that response was answered by a man who was not looking for a babysitter. The girl's brother took her to meet the man, they exchanged names and phone numbers – obviously not the perpetrator's real name and number -- and then the girl and man drove away. She was found murdered just a few days later. Parents everywhere across our town were instantly very protective of their children, especially young, teen girls. I know my own parents emphasized over and over that I was never to put my name and specifics anywhere in a public place like a laundromat. I can't remember if the man was apprehended or not, I just remember the horror of a teen-ager like myself innocently thinking she was going to a job but ending up instead being a murder victim. It was tragic, but it definitely left an impact on my life.

Also, it wasn't only our city with the worse than tragic news, but my cousin and her family also witnessed their city's own catastrophe while living in Oregon. It was not news of a murder, but news of devastation from a flood. "When we were back in Tennessee during Christmas of 1964, Douglas County area suffered a terrible flood. Our house was on the North Umpqua River, and nearly destroyed. I remember watching TV at my grandmother's house with the news about the flood. We saw the watermark one inch above the door facing in the family room, and about four feet of mud/silt through the house. As a kid, you don't get that involved; however, I can't imagine how my parents felt…starting over after the flood of that magnitude."

Of course on the lighter side of the news, The Beatles came to America, Days of Our Lives made its debut, and space travel was coming on the scene with the culmination of a man landing on the moon and setting the American flag on its surface by the end of the decade. In the words of Kathy Steenson, "Visions of the moon would never be the same. We had proof that it was not made of cheese." It was that thought as well as the mantra that could be heard from kids and adults as well, "Whoever lands on the moon will rule the world." Carol also thought the moon landing was interesting; however, "it was boring in comparison to Lost in Space."

Telstar, the first commercial satellite, made its appearance. It was the first device to relay phone calls and fax images and television pictures. It didn't last long in space but from it, came what we have today.

In addition to the moon landing, and not quite the world-wide viewing of President Kennedy, Carol also remembers when President Eisenhower passed away and watching his funeral on her grandmother's black and white TV.

The first Wal-Mart opened in Arkansas, Six Flags first opened in Texas with an admitting price of $2.75 per person, Betty Friedan founded NOW organization, and the Ken doll came on the scene to match up with Barbie.

Hollywood was getting in the news with the first Hollywood Walk of Fame star being put in place. Is there a memory for who that might be? It was Joanna Woodward, the wife of Paul Newman – Hollywood's greatest leading man with those piercing, gorgeous blue eyes! Sidney Poitier made news by being the first black performer to receive the award of Best Actor, and Ben Hur was nominated for the Best Picture.

Books and Comics also made the news headlines with Pulitzer prize winner, Harper Lee, publishing <u>To Kill a Mockingbird</u> – after being rejected nearly one hundred times -- and Spiderman making his debut. Of course, the Spiderman edition would transform comics from playful Archie and Casper the Friendly Ghost to what they are today with all types of action figures committing a multitude of horrendous acts on their victims.

The Ford Mustang was produced and sold, the designing of the mini skirt became a fashion craze, and the Smiley Face button made its debut. Other medicines, food, technology, and fun to enter our world was Valium, non-dairy creamer, soft contact lenses, hand held calculators, the IBM Selectric typewriter, the artificial heart, and the audio cassette.

Prices then seemed at a complete low compared to the prices of today:

- Income - $5,315.00
- Medium house - $12,700.00
- New car - $2,600.00
- Gas - $.25
- Movie ticket - $.25
- Stamp - $.04
- Milk - $.49 ½ gallon
- Coffee - $.10 - $.15
- Eggs - $.57
- Ground Beef - $.49

Extra Thoughts:

College campus riots

Viet Nam protests

"I have a dream"

Swearing in of Lyndon Johnson

Fallout Shelters

Cold War

Cassius Clay

Charles Manson

First Man on the Moon

The Good Side of Memory

The house on Lenox. My window is the top right.

My parents and Mrs. Williams in front of our house on a "work day."

The warmth of Mrs. Williams's kitchen was a gathering many times. My dad in the foreground, Mrs. Williams in the background, David standing. Bubba hiding behind my dad.

Mrs. Rapisardi thirteen years later.

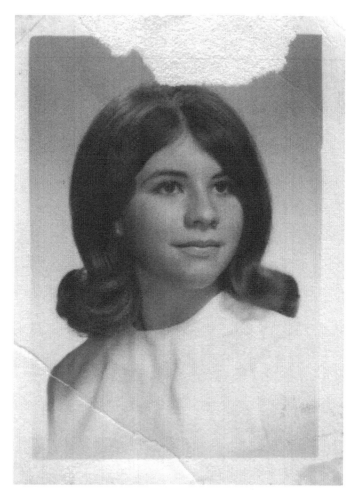

Paula Rapisardi O'Connor -- "The Girl"

Bubba Williams - The Boy Next Door

The usual summer excursion to the beach.

Bubba (L), Nicki (M), David (R).

The Good Side of Memory

David (L), Bubba, and friend wrestle on the beach.

*Life long friends of fifty-five years.
Paula O'Connor (L) and Marty Matthews (R)*

V

Friends

Because of my numerous moves as a "Navy brat," I had to make new friends often and rather quickly. While I can look back over the course of the years with my parents and all our moves, Lenox Avenue afforded me to make the best friends – a special one that would last a life time – specifically friends that I would never forget. These friends on Lenox Avenue – four girls – were ones that were in my life daily. I cannot remember a day that we didn't see each other during those years. Perhaps it wasn't all four at the same time, but at least one or two – many times all four -- were with me during the course of the day! Factor in Bubba, the boy next door, David from two streets over, as well as Loyall M. from one street over, and we had quite the fun, talks, and memories.

As I mentioned previously, one of the girls, Paula Rapisardi O'Connor, became a friend that has lasted a life time. The other two, Kathy B., and Glenda T., lost touch with Paula and me over the course of time.

We saw them once perhaps twenty-five years ago, but then we lost touch completely. Nevertheless, the memories we had of the years on Lenox Avenue have lasted a life time.

A specific note – Paula and I became friends first at the age of ten years – "the girl" on the bicycle -- and it wasn't until about two years later that we met Kathy and the "gang." We just happened to be walking down Lenox Avenue, and Kathy, Bubba, and some others were outside talking in Kathy's yard. At that time, Bubba and his family lived across the street from Kathy, and they hadn't moved next door to me yet. From that evening on – August 3, 1962 – it was a bond and memories with all of us that lasted decades.

The beginning of the 60s became known as a simple time. Riding bicycles, listening to records, walking to the beach, and just being together. In 2016, we wouldn't have said chilling or chillaxing, but that is exactly what we did. Much of our times together took place at my house since that seemed to be the central place and, of course, I had boys living next door! And what fun we had because of the boys next door. Paula and I share a specific vivid memory that I'm sure Kathy and Glenda would say they do too if they were together with us now. The memory entails we four girls going upstairs in my house to the bathroom. We had the light turned out, and we went to the bathroom window – to spy! We looked out and directly across the way (approximately ten feet) was the window of Bubba's attic. We were spying because, as it happened on any given night, many of the boys were shooting pool in the attic. It could have been the many nights while parents enjoyed conversations on the front lawn – we enjoyed spying. Since it happened quite frequently, we would watch – generally from my front yard – to see when the guys went into Bubba's house. Once we saw them go in, we always ran into my house, directly up to the bathroom to see if they were shooting pool. I laugh now as I think of how we had our four heads stuck together in the dark bathroom, looking out the window, watching every move they made. Though it was never said, I cannot imagine now that the boys didn't know we were watching them. Most likely, they enjoyed it as much as we did!

Some enjoyment of the pool playing in the attic

one day came to a halt when one of the boys stuck his foot through the kitchen ceiling, which was directly under the attic where the pool table sat. The flooring wasn't completely finished in the attic, and there were only boards placed sporadically along the floor where one could walk. Gingerly the boys would walk around, making sure they stepped on boards and not on the dry wall! It must have been an exciting game because one of the neighboring boys stepped backwards and stepped right through the ceiling. I can remember the angst Bubba and his brother, Bobby, felt at having to show Mrs. Williams the hole in the ceiling when she came home from work. By evening, after witnessing the hole and talking of nothing else all day, Paula and I left so that Bubba and Bobby could meet Mrs. Williams walking home from the bus stop to tell her the devastating news before she arrived at the house. Needless to say, she wasn't a happy camper! Though I don't remember if he did, it seems that Mr. Rapisardi helped in fixing the hole for Mrs. Williams – like I said, neighbors helped neighbors!

The absolute best memory, though, or so I

thought over the years after I moved away, was New Year's Eve, 1963, when we went to Bubba's house to listen to records and dance. Mrs. Williams had goodies made, we had cokes to drink, and had plenty of records to play. We laughed, ate, danced, and were thrilled when midnight came and were able to muster up a peck or two on the lips. I believe we girls walked on air for the next two weeks and talked of nothing else. I don't know about the boys, but the girls had never been kissed. It was a first for us, and, for me, I fell in love that much more!

Most summer days were spent at the beach, which was a few blocks from Lenox Avenue. At any given time, there were five, eight, ten, kids walking to the beach to spend the day, burying each other in the sand, throwing each other in the water, and simply lying on the beach, trying to get the best tan possible. Of course the girls always slathered on the baby oil because that is what produced the "best tan," or so we thought. I doubt that is what the people making sunscreen would have said!

Kathy Steenson and her friends were also beach people, preferring it over their own pool in their back yard. She even dreamed of a loftier event at the beach – surfing! "We pretended to "practice surf" because the waves on Miami Beach were small. We could only dream of actually surfing like they did in California and Hawaii." For us on Lenox Avenue, it was a walk to the beach but for Kathy and her friends, it was much longer. "But well worth it!" she emphasized. "From my house to South Beach was a three-bus ride, but once my friends joined me at the bus station, it was chatter and laughter all the way."

As one who lived many years near the ocean, there is something about the beach that causes its preference over a pool or the lake. For me, it was the sound of the waves hitting the shore, the good, clean feeling of sand under my feet, and the running as fast as possible into the water and jumping in, screaming all the way. A pool just didn't afford me those benefits, and my friends and I thought of "beach" never "pool" when summertime rolled around. Kathy Steenson felt that same way. "Our new house had four bedrooms, two bathrooms, and a pool. At first the pool was a highlight of living in Miami, but eventually the newness wore off, and I preferred to go to the beach with my friends."

Where we "Lenox Kids" walked to a specific portion of the beach, directly in front of it was the amusement park. As a side, I believe a movie was made of this amusement park years ago; specifically, about the roller coaster. It was a wooden roller coaster – perhaps none made like it anymore – and it ultimately was torn down. Though we all had ridden on it, it was rickety and in need of being torn down. When the ride began and the coaster cars would ascend to the top, the noise of the wooden creaking and moving could be heard all the way back to Lenox Avenue. Of course, by 2016 the entire amusement park has disappeared and a family park is now in its place. As families sit at picnic tables today, they have no idea of the fun that inhabited that same area fifty years ago.

While at the beach, if any one of us became tired of sand and water, we walked through the amusement park for a change of scenery. We didn't ride any of the rides – that was done at night when we specifically decided to go to the amusement park itself -- but we would grab a drink or two or perhaps something to eat. There was always something to do; always someone with whom to walk. Sometimes it was fun just to sit on one of the amusement park benches and talk – I cherished those times.

Evenings during the summer brought out records and dancing in our garage. My parents generally had cola drinks and, like I mentioned before, Mother always had baked goods. We stayed until parents sent kids home or other parents called for their own child to come home. We danced, sang, laughed, played silly games, and just had good, simple fun.

When we took a break from dancing or playing the silly games – slips of paper in a bowl with instructions written on each one, i.e., you have to walk to the stop sign holding hands with someone you like – we listened to Dave Gardner's humorous album. It had stories he told from Julius Caesar to motorcycle rides to himself as a boy. Again, simple times but fun times.

One evening that stands out as another vivid memory was the time my dad brought out his slides to show everyone. For many not knowing or having never seen slides, they were hard little pictures that were put into a projector with the image then focused on a screen. My dad had about five hours of slides, and he was always excited to show them. That particular evening, it seems everyone had come over to hang out, realizing it was going to be "movie" night. All the boys as well as the girls were sitting on chairs, couches, and the floor watching the screen as my dad showed slides and talked about each one. Then the one slide came up of a statue of King David. As many have seen in books, King David may or may not have had his clothes on. In this particular slide, he didn't have clothes on, and was shown "anatomically correct." It was a surprise to my dad when he pushed in the projector arm to bring up the image on the screen, but when he did, there was complete silence in the room. Suddenly, someone snickered, and the room erupted into laughter — including my dad! Who knows what someone would say in 2016 about that slide and my dad showing it, but in 1960, it was innocent and the only thing that ensued was uproarious laughter!

Whether we all spent an evening watching slides,

listening to records, or just talking among ourselves, the friendship among us four girls was one of being inseparable. If one of the girls came to one house, we two would begin looking for the other two to join us. Of course since Paula and I lived across the street from one another, we saw each other more often, and it was like Bubba said these many years later, "When you saw one (Paula), you saw the other (me).

Often times, generally at night, we four girls became silly, and we would link arms in the middle of Lenox Avenue, and go skipping down the road singing, "We're off to see the Wizard, the wonderful Wizard of Oz!" Two blocks down Lenox, there was a house being built, and we always thought we heard something or saw something we didn't want to, and we would come running, screaming back down the street. Nothing was ever there, and the four of us would collapse in our yard in peals of laughter. A good many of those times brought Bubba out of his house, and he would stay with us and talk. I think about it now, and it wasn't too bad that a boy of his age (16 years) had the attention of four girls on a daily basis.

Sometimes it wasn't the house down the road that scared us but Bubba himself. Many times when we four girls were in the yard talking and or doing whatever, he would jump out from the bushes and yell. We would end up screaming and running, then, again, collapsing in peals of laughter.

The back yard of my house led right out onto the golf course, separated only by a small ditch, which could easily be jumped over. A few steps passed a couple of trees, and we were on the 5th green of the course. Many times we would play on the fairway of the course after dusk when all golfers no longer played. We walked the fairway, and, if Bubba let us use one of his clubs, we would attempt to hit the ball from tee to green. While we girls were just hitting a ball around on the fairway for fun, Bubba was the true golfer. In his own words, "I loved to play golf." He was actually practicing each time he went out on the fairway as he was on the high school golf team. Coming out one evening with us, my dad asked Bubba to show him a swing or two. He did, and from then on, my dad was hooked. Until my dad's death, he played the game almost every day!

While we all used clubs and hit balls, attempting to play golf, David enjoyed sneaking around the fairways – possibly while we actually hit balls, but possibly whenever he could – grabbing balls, then selling them. Other than "playing" golf on the fairway – or sneaking around -- Paula vividly remembers the big snow and all of us having a snowball fight on the fairway. Hiding behind the small hills, the trees, and in the ditch, or just running and throwing snowballs at each other. The boys plummeted the girls while we tried to get a few hits in ourselves, however it was on that cold day on the fairway, the big snow left a huge memory.

If it weren't golf, or the occasional snowball fight, we would play badminton without a net, counting how many times we would hit the birdie back and forth to each other before it hit the ground. Sometimes the "game" would get rough, and accusations of not trying to hit the birdie to another person came about. Typically, though, it was all in fun, and we enjoyed counting hits, seeing, of course, who could hit the most.

While skateboarding was unheard of in that era,

we fashioned our own – or I should say the boys fashioned a skateboard, and we girls attempted to use it. It was a short board with a skate pulled in half with wheels attached to the bottom of the front and wheels attached to the back of the board. It obviously wasn't as nice as the ones they have today in 2016, and our board had a tendency to turn and flip the person off, but we all spent many hours on the skateboard going up and down Lenox Avenue. Many skinned knees and elbows that summer!

Our skateboards were fashioned simply as was Fred and his dad's go cart. It was fashioned out of one inch angle wire for the frame and then equipped with a seat, pedals, steering wheel, and a lawnmower motor on the back. Oh yes, we used our imaginations in every sense of the word!

There was also the time of the pogo stick – again counting how many times a person could jump – hopefully, more times than the next person. I attempted jumping on a pogo stick recently, and my feet never cooperated – one always missed and I had to jump off the stick. It was easy to do in 1960, not so much when IN your sixties.

The yoyo brought out more competition with who could perform walking the dog, around the world, or baby in the cradle without losing control. Then there was the hula hoop! Everyone thought he/she could hula hoop around the waist, neck, arm, or leg! Who could go the longest or who had the most times around each body part dominated the hula hoop craze! And the craze was everywhere! Jon said, "I participated in a hula hoop marathon on the courthouse yard in Bedford for four hours until the hoop slipped to my knees. I then continued another hour. Suffice it to say, I could hardly walk the next day with all the bruises."

Surprisingly, there was never a time of football, baseball, or basketball on Lenox Avenue. None of us had any of those balls or a goal in which to throw them. Despite not playing the games on Lenox, Bubba and his school friends did attend football games, and at church, he played softball on the church league. Also, Paula and I went to basketball games where she attended elementary school; however, I think we really went to see her friend, Patty M., cheer at the games rather than watch the basketball games themselves.

David played sandlot ball and marbles with Bubba and other friends on the street where he lived. The lone girl in their group, known as the tom boy on his street, shot marbles with them. Unfortunately for them, she always beat them and took all their marbles, something he and the other guys found humiliating and embarrassing! Also for him, there were the trips to the turtle pond to catch turtles.

Fred and his friends didn't go to a turtle pond but to a swamp where they swam, boated, and frog gigged. "At any given time while we swam, someone would yell, 'Snake!' and everyone would swim as fast as possible trying to get out of the swamp. Was there a snake? Sometimes yes, sometimes no, but we never took the chance to look – just swam as fast as we could getting out of there".

In their small boat – again in the swamp – Fred and a friend would shoot snakes with a .22 rifle for fun. Fred remembers one time his friend sitting in the front "look-out" seat with his feet perched on the boat's edge and his rifle between his legs searching for snakes. "He saw one, shot at it, and grazed its head.

The snake reared up out of the water, circled, then started for the boat. At first we were laughing while the snake went around in circles, but once it started for the boat, that changed everything. My "look out" shooter started screaming, 'Paddle! Paddle!' Unfortunately, because we had dropped our makeshift anchor, and because of the axe handle I was using as a paddle, we got nowhere. The boat stayed exactly where it was before the shot was fired! The snake swam right up to the boat and bit – head first – 'smack' right where my friend had just removed his feet. Our hearts pounded, and I was still trying to paddle as fast as I could with the axe handle. But all of a sudden the snake fell back into the water and swam away. We looked at each other, gathered our wits, pulled up our make shift anchor, and paddled to the bank. Shooting was over." Did snakes cause them to stay away? No! Nighttime brought out the new games.

"Frog gigging was a nighttime pleasure with a three-pronged gig fashioned to some type of pole – even a broom stick. Once again in our infamous boat, we had flashlights in hand as our lights skimmed across the water – bingo! Frog! Wide-eyed looking right at us – well, looking into the light actually. We then speared the frog, maneuvered it into the boat – without dropping it off the end of the gig -- and looked for more. Once we had enough and were back on ground, we would cook 'em all in a Crisco can."

Not so much into snakes or frogs – or turtles -- many times we four girls would simply find ourselves walking around the block talking and visiting neighbors that we encountered. Brenda also walked around her block with her best friend listening to a portable radio. While this isn't that much unlike the young generation of 2016, in the 1960s, we didn't have ear plugs to hear only our music, but we also interacted with friends and neighbors along the way while listening to music.

Listening to records and listening to the radio encompassed a great deal of our time, and, because of that, we four girls attempted to write our own song so that we could turn the lyrics in to a specific rock n roll singer. This singer used to perform at our local concert venue, and our big hope was that he would like the lyrics and would sing our song at one of his performances. Our song was destined to be a hit – or so we thought! It was entitled, "That's All I Need," and the only lyrics I can remember are from the first verse:

> This don't have to be true love,
> Just to hold me in your arms
> And to thrill me with your charms,
> That's all I need.

Obviously, verses and pages were filled with more "love" lyrics; unfortunately, we never made it to the place where the singer performed, and our number one hit song, never hit the charts – it just became another good memory.

Music and dancing seemed to be as popular in the 1960s as it is today, including when Carolyn lived overseas. She went to their teen club, traveling on the military bus – all without her parents. As it was with Paula and me – we walked or rode bicycles everywhere with no fear – Carolyn said, "There was no evil, and we could go anyplace with much freedom." Incidentally, though, she and her friends had plenty of music to listen to, but what she did miss while living overseas was "real" milk. "We could not get real milk for the two years we were in Japan, only reconstituted. We couldn't get enough whole milk to drink when we arrived back home."

Interesting discussions ensued among the four of us girls, one about which I vividly recall – religion! I was the only Baptist, and the other three girls were Catholic. At the ages of thirteen and fourteen, passions can run high, but most likely, a good many of the thoughts and words came from our parents. It was quite similar with Kathy Schlegel. "Our neighbors were Protestant and Republican. We were Catholic and Democrat. Rocky beginning, but then I became accepted with girls my own age and remember many games of Canasta on the patio."

Yes, talks of religion could get quite heated – even back in the 1960s. Jon said, "My parents were Protestant and Republican, and I had a playmate who was Catholic and Italian. We got into a spat one day over the gowns priests wore. Our mothers finally had to straighten out the misunderstanding."

While I went to the Baptist church – with Bubba and his brother, Bobby – I did attend Paula's Catholic church occasionally, and I always found it very interesting. A good bit of the talking – I don't know if they called it a sermon or not – was done in Latin, and I really didn't know what was being said. The parishioners also stood up and sat down far more than we did at the Baptist church. In fact, before entering the pew row where I would sit with Paula and her family, we genuflected – I learned that word early from Paula, but had never heard it mentioned in the Baptist church – then we went into the row and sat down. The service was different, but I enjoyed the times I went with Paula and her family.

Whether Sunday services or everyday getting together, we girls thoroughly enjoyed whatever we did. Lynn was slightly older in her memories with being able to cruise with her boyfriend around the fast food place. She also went steady and wrapped boys' rings in angora so they would fit her finger. She also remembered, "Sneaking into the drive-in with two boys in the trunk just to see if we could get away with it. I might add, it wasn't my idea – I am a follower not a leader!"

We four also talked about boys, but none of us went steady, and none of us had a ring to wear on any of our fingers from a boy. We did go to the movies, but it was in a theater. We never went to a drive-in, but we probably would have liked to have done so. Our ages ranged from thirteen to fifteen years, so I believe we were too young for any of that.

Talking, laughing, walking, and listening to music with girlfriends seemed the norm during the 1960s, but that obviously was a "girl" thing because Chris found entirely different activities. "Swimming or fishing in Feather River or Butte Creek the creek was a daily activity in the summer. Working on cars was a year-round activity, as was exploring the surrounding foothills, either by car, pickup truck, or on foot."

Not to be outdone in the Olympics, Fred and his friends practiced pole vaulting using bamboo canes. "We never had a fear that anyone would impale himself if the cane broke. We would just run, stick the cane to the ground, and pole vault over other canes fashioned together that made the vault itself." I had to smile at his story because the closest we girls ever came to pole vaulting – and possibly hurting ourselves -- was two of us holding a pole (broom stick or something else) at each end while the other two did the limbo under it.

From a young "pre-tween" girl at that time, Carol's activities included some innocent fun: "Played with dolls, set up my Suzy Homemaker appliances under the mimosa tree outside to play house, explored the creek throughout the neighborhood and coming home covered in mud, picked the honeysuckle down by the creek, climbed tees, and listened to my grandmother's stories about her childhood, sitting with her on her patio swing."

Lali also played with paper dolls up and until she was twelve years old. "Along with the dolls, we made furniture out of our mom's small jewelry gift boxes."

Rather than small jewelry boxes, Jan and her twin sister fashioned a stable full of "stick" horses. "We also had a whole 'village' cleared out in the woods – complete with our imaginary house, a store, a church, etc. We named it Centerville."

With my three friends, Paula, Kathy, and Glenda, I remember our special times together as did so many others with friends of their own. It was a wonderful time of innocence, simplicity, imagination, and naiveté – one that will never be forgotten, and one that truly brought out the good side of memory!

Extra Thoughts:

Pen Pals

Hide and Seek

Scary movies

Cokes in a tea room

Sliding down dry grass hillsides on cardboard

Marbles

Flying kites

Sock Hops

Banana Bike Seats

Chatty Cathy

Tiny Tears

Jacks

Granny beads (would have left a line around the necks formed by sweat and dirt from playing outside all day.

Easy Bake Oven

Twister

G I Joe

Marty Matthews

Hula Hoops

Pinball Machines

Candyland

Mood Rings

Dippidy Doo

Noxzema

Skinny Dip Perfume

Garter Belt/no Panty Hose

Head Scarves

Culottes

Shift Dresses

Mary Jane Shoes

Brownie Camera

Drive-in Movies

The Draft

Ipana Toothpaste

Halo Shampoo

Prell Shampoo'

Gleam Toothpaste

Spoolies

Curb sitting and talking

Cherry Cokes

VI

The Boy Next Door

In 2016 it's hard to understand the simplicity of the time in the 1960s, and a teen today would most likely find events, situations, boy/girl relationships rather silly in comparison. While teens today are far more mature in thought and actions than teens in the 1960s, for us growing up during that era we were really ensconced in naiveté. The Boy Next Door and the upcoming Lifetime Friend (next chapter) are perfect examples of innocence and what I would call a sweetness between friends that doesn't quite exist today as it did fifty years ago.

No one made a bigger impact on my life during this time than Bubba Williams, the boy next door. I met him at twelve years, just short of thirteen – a teen-ager. He had already hit that mark by two years and upon seeing him that night on Lenox Avenue – August 3, 1962 -- talking and laughing, it was obvious, I had fallen for an "older guy." A tall, slender, and good-looking older guy. Normally, my parents would have discouraged that immediately, but they adored Bubba once they met him and his family. Okay, okay! They thought he was a nice guy; I adored Bubba.

Once we met Bubba and the new friends, Paula and I found ourselves walking a block or two down Lenox Avenue – where we had never ventured before – daily in search of Kathy and Bubba. At this same time, we had met Glenda, but the memory eludes me as to how that came about. However it did, we four girls became fast friends, and the boys, Bubba, David, and Loyall, (the last two also on the street that night) seemed to be right in the thick of things with us.

Within weeks after meeting, it seemed, Bubba and his family moved into the empty house next door to ours. Needless to say, I couldn't have been happier. When I say my parents thought he was a nice guy, that was quite true. Bubba seemed to become a part of our lives from the start, coming to our house, talking with me and my parents, and, most importantly, teaching my dad how to play golf. Even if it hadn't been for golf, my dad said many times, "Now that is one smart boy!" So, definitely, my parents, especially my dad, liked Bubba.

I don't know how it came about that my dad was even interested in golf, but one day he had purchased golf clubs, and he and Bubba were going out the back of our house onto the golf course after hours so they could practice. From just practicing out back on the 5th fairway, it became serious enough that I soon found my dad and Bubba going to different golf courses to play rounds together. What would be the obvious? I found that I loved the game of golf, and I wanted to be able to play too.

Once that decision was made, Bubba and I found ourselves walking the golf course fairway after hours on a good many evenings. Oftentimes, it was with our friends or my dad, but Bubba and I did do a great deal of walking and talking alone. For me, simply walking and talking with Bubba was such an enjoyable time, but it was those nights I especially liked when we sat on the green talking way after dark. The hours we talked, I cannot remember one conversation. I just remember how much I relished those evenings.

Because I said I wanted to learn to play golf (seriously, I did like the game itself!), Bubba taught me how to swing, putt, and effectively hold the club.

That, of course, was the most enjoyable part since he had to bring his arms around me to show me how to hold the club. I am sure that I liked that far more than he did!

One memorable night, which was pretty much in line with the foot through the ceiling while the boys were playing pool in the attic, Bubba and I were walking down the fairway after he had hit his ball. It was dusk, we were talking, not paying attention to anything, and he was swinging his golf club in his hand nonchalantly. I heard a noise – perhaps his gasp of surprise, I don't remember but a definite "thunk." He had swung the club accidentally up to his mouth and hit his front tooth. I had continued walking, most likely talking to myself; but he had stopped. I turned around to see him standing awkwardly with his mouth gaped open. As I stared at him, he said, "I knocked my tooth out." Neither one of us could believe it, and to say he was miserable would be an understatement. I don't remember him being in pain, but I do remember him feeling pretty wretched because he thought he had done something so foolish. Both of us, him feeling forlorn, me feeling hurt and sorry for him, walked slowly and wordlessly back to his house. I wanted to comfort him, but I honestly didn't know what to say other than, "I'm so sorry."

Of course, his biggest concern was going home and telling his mom that he had been swinging his club and had knocked out part of his tooth. A costly dentist visit would be on the horizon, something neither he nor his mom had a desire to have done. Subsequently, the tooth was fixed, and I saw no difference in his smile. Whatever the dentist had to do – most likely crowning the tooth – he did it well. Practicing our golf shots took on a new meaning after that evening. The club being used was to be kept close to the ground when walking! No swinging clubs allowed!

Those practicing days of golf took my dad and me into the future of playing golf, sometime on a daily basis. Once he retired from the Navy, he played golf almost every day with his brother and other friends that enjoyed the game as much as he did. I, too, played golf as often as possible, sometimes as much as twice a day when scrambles with groups were involved. Those days of practicing and my playing so often paid off because I, and a favorite partner of mine, won a Lads and Lassies Tournament in Kentucky.

I don't know if Bubba still plays golf or not, but my dad and I played up and until he passed away. Once he passed away, my clubs were retired as were his. No longer walking and practicing on a fairway with Bubba, no longer playing with my dad, and no longer living in Kentucky playing golf with friends, I didn't have that desire to play as I had before. I still have his pride and joy, though – a set of Ben Hogan golf clubs that have never been used and that are still stored in the box in which they were purchased.

During the 1960s, as I mentioned previously, paperboys used to throw papers on porches then go around collecting money every two weeks. Bubba was the paperboy for the afternoon paper, "The Ledger Star," on Lenox Avenue and other surrounding areas, while someone else threw the morning paper, "The Virginian Pilot." He would fold the papers or wrap them with a rubber band near a store, High's Ice Cream, where the papers were delivered. Of course, Paula and I needed to have an ice cream cone just about every day from High's. Often times, once we had our cones, we could be found talking to Bubba while he folded his papers and placed them in his bicycle basket, before throwing them.

Today in 2016, if the newspaper is still being delivered in various areas, it is done by someone driving a car and depositing said newspaper in a newspaper box usually found beside the mailbox. Gone are the bicycles with huge baskets on the front for throwing papers, as well as, heaven forbid, the satchels carried on the backs of the paperboys. The satchels were horribly heavy as were the bicycles with the baskets. They were not the easiest to handle when all the papers were rolled and stacked inside the basket. I don't think I could have picked up the bicycle, let alone guide it and ride it, when the basket was loaded down with all the papers.

Occasionally, when Paula didn't go with me to High's, I would go there and talk with Bubba then walk with him while he threw the papers. Either he would pedal slowly as I walked beside him – that had to be a feat in itself with all the papers in the basket -- or he would walk his bicycle while the two of us walked together. Many times I collected the bi-monthly money from his customers with him and enjoyed the time of ambling down Lenox, talking with him. I also respected and appreciated him in the way he talked and interacted with his customers – mannerly, friendly, always with a smile on his face. This would be whether he received his required money or not. He never let it affect his attitude with his customers.

We had many talks together, not only on the golf course or while he threw papers and collected monies, but also while sitting on his porch in the evenings when everyone else had gone home. Again, I cannot remember what we talked about, but they were times, like sitting on the green on the golf course, that I cherished. He reminded me not long ago that on those nights when we would talk that I would sometimes scratch his back. Oh yes, I remembered. I have to smile now thinking about that time and how sweet for me those moments were. Just sayin' – I was a young girl totally enamored with the boy next door!

So enamored that I was thrilled when Bubba

had surgery, and I had to play "nurse" during his recovery. Neither one of us can remember why he had surgery or what the surgery entailed; nevertheless, I agreed readily those many years ago to take care of him when the doctor had said he would have to have someone to stay with him while he recovered. Since Mrs. Williams worked and his brother, Bobby, probably did too at that time, Bubba offered my services, and I readily agreed.

My "nursing duties" required making sure Bubba had something to eat as well as helping him around the house when he walked. I went to his house before lunch and was able to make soup or sandwiches – obviously something easy since I didn't do much around the kitchen myself. He did admonish me, though, because of the way I made peanut butter sandwiches. It appeared I didn't put enough peanut butter on the slices of bread – and, Bubba, if you're reading this, I still don't put much peanut butter on the bread!

It wasn't only talking, "nursing duties," and the like, but many times I would find myself at Bubba's house just listening to records with him and his older brother, Bobby. While Bobby, and it seemed Bubba as well, enjoyed records like The Ventures – guitar music and such – I preferred "real" rock n roll! Nevertheless, I feigned pretense and listened to The Ventures with them, saying how much I enjoyed their music. I even asked to borrow the record so I could listen to it at my house – I didn't really listen to it when I went home, but I thought it sounded good when I was asking to borrow it. My thoughts were, "How impressed they would be that I liked their music."

Recently, I watched The Ventures on YouTube performing "Hawaii Five-O." I closed my eyes, and I could almost feel the years drifting away back to a much younger time. But then, that's what music does – it takes the years away, to the time when the song is first heard, evoking wonderful memories. Not really surprising, I found, then, that I actually enjoyed listening to The Ventures in my older years!

On Sundays, I didn't feign pretense -- like I did about music -- when going to church with Bubba and Bobby, saying that I liked to do so. It was something I thoroughly enjoyed, and, to this day, I am eternally grateful to them for taking me each Sunday. My love for the Lord has increased many times over since those days, and I wouldn't have gone to church had it not been for those two special guys. I cannot remember if we walked or if Bobby drove us, but each Sunday morning, the three of us went together.

One specific time I remember anticipating a Sunday was before an Easter service. I would be wearing heels for the first time, and I was extremely nervous. My mother had bought me my heels weeks before, and I had practiced walking in them on a daily basis. Every time I was in the house by myself, I practiced walking in them because I was so afraid that I would fall, trip, stumble, something embarrassing for a young girl! I made it, though, that Easter Sunday without tripping, and I felt so grown up, so mature to be able to go to church in heels and hose like my mother when she dressed up. It was truly special because I enjoyed every Sunday morning seeing Bubba looking especially handsome coming to pick me up, but in my heels that first time on Easter Sunday, I felt as pretty as he was handsome. Oh, the days of young love!

As I mentioned before, the days spent at the beach were plentiful! It was a short trek many of us made daily during the summer months. Typically, it would have been at least three of the guys and three of us girls since Glenda never went as much as Kathy, Paula, and I did. I do not remember that Bubba and I ever went alone, but we always went with the "gang." To me, it mattered not – we were all together, and we were all having fun! The most fun was being thrown in the water despite how we girls screamed for the boys not do so. At any given time, the boys would heft us over their shoulders, pick us up and carry us, or two would pick us up by our arms and feet and "swing" carry us out to the water and throw us in. Screaming, "No, No, No" all the way, we were secretly loving every minute of it.

Fun seemed to be the main pastime, but Bubba and I also went to school – I was in junior high, and Bubba was in high school. While one might think he would have helped me with homework or the like, I never remember that happening with one exception – the dissection of the frog. Why I was having to dissect the frog at home in the first place, I don't know. Perhaps our science class required that as "homework," I'm really not sure; nevertheless, my complaints of having to do it as well as smelling the ghastly odor of formaldehyde, made Bubba say, "I'll help."

We took the frog and everything out from its package and bottle on the counter in my kitchen – atop old newspapers -- and he actually did the dissecting. I wrote down all findings. Whatever I had to do took longer than either of us thought, and he had to go home and eat before coming back and finishing the dissection. When he did come back – perhaps green around the edges, I don't know – he said, "Well, I couldn't eat my dinner tonight." I looked perplexed and asked why. He said it was fried chicken and every chicken leg looked like what he had just cut apart on my kitchen counter. I smile now thinking about it, and the way he looked when he came back to my house – stomach somewhat upset -- only to start dissecting again.

He was quite the guy, whether just talking, having fun, or dissecting a nasty frog to help me with my homework. Yes, it was such a wonderful, sweet time, and in my thirteen/fourteen year old mind – spent with Bubba, it was the best!

VII

Lifetime friend: Paula Rapisardi O'Connor

Paula and I were both in elementary school when we met – watching each other on a bicycle, riding up and down Lenox Avenue. Too young to actually walk across the street to the other one's house and introduce ourselves, we rode a few days alone, glancing at each other out of the corner of our eyes. Whoever was first, I cannot remember, but we finally stopped riding and talked. From that moment on, we became instant friends – friends that have lasted over decades, five decades as a matter of fact.

I smile now as I think about that day of long ago when we first met. We had to tell each other everything about ourselves: our friends from school (we attended different schools), all about our families, what we liked to do, and especially where we wanted to ride our bicycles. Regarding schools, I went to a public school, and Paula went to a Catholic school. If nothing else, I loved the uniform that she had to wear every day – a plaid skirt, white blouse, and matching knee socks. She always looked so put-together and so cute in her uniform. My clothes were okay, and I liked what I wore, but I especially liked her uniform.

In the beginning, we spent hours riding on our bicycles. To two young girls in our tweens, as they would call us in 2016, we thought we were riding miles from Lenox Avenue, and said so many times. In reality, we were a good distance from Lenox, but we were probably not miles away. Nevertheless, we rode our bicycles constantly and, we were like David, who said he rode into "strange" neighborhoods, checking everything and everyone out.

If Paula and I weren't bike riding, we were walking. Of course, there was the exception when we rode the city bus downtown, which really WAS quite a distance for two young girls. In that era, though, it was not even thought to be from our parents, "Oh my gosh, what might happen?" Because the answer would be, "Nothing!"

On the city bus the day we road downtown, we rode, we found the correct bus stop, we walked, and found the exact place for which we were looking.

On that specific day, we actually received our social security cards while downtown. It doesn't seem feasible that two ten or eleven year olds could or would be able to ride that distance, find the stop, and then find the office for social security in 2016. Fifty years ago, it was a different time and a different mindset for young girls and adults as well.

Before meeting Bubba and the others, Paula and I, by ourselves, walked to the beach, the amusement park, the theater to watch movies – at a cost of $.25 – the stores, and the library. The amusement park was directly in front of the beach – once crossing the boardwalk from the beach, one could walk right into the amusement park. Where we always went to the beach, the first ride once crossing the boardwalk and coming into the amusement park was The Twister. Invariably, we would stop and watch others while they rode and screamed during the ride. We didn't ride rides that much, but we would walk through the amusement park if we became hot or thirsty to find something to eat or drink. Probably more of the sweets that Mr. Rapisardi didn't like Paula having – cotton candy, caramel apples, cokes, and more. It was definitely a sweetaholic's paradise at the park. The rest of time, we stayed on the beach, played in the water, and became really tanned. Not that we were there to get a tan because, we thought, writing in the wet sand or playing in the water was the purpose for going to the beach, but we certainly had that sun glow about us!

Not only did we make many trips to the beach, theater, and stores, but we also made far more to the library. As soon as school ended and summer was upon us, we began our trips to the library. Of course, when my mother was working there, we were able to go into the back of the library, marked "employees only," and visit with her and some of the other ladies. I always found it enjoyable to go in the back where other patrons could not go. Perhaps it was just that special feeling of being allowed to do something as a child that no one else could do; whatever the case, Paula and I both enjoyed being in the back, talking to the ladies.

Paula and I checked out book after book, and we spent many days reading and talking about our books. That love for reading, which started even before we met, has lasted well into our adult years as we both are still avid readers, both being members of book clubs; she being a member of two book clubs! Not only an avid reader, Paula is a dedicated reader now in her adult years. She sets her alarm for 5:30 a.m. daily so she can read before starting her day. Now that is dedication and a love for books!

Along with reading them, we also wrote stories. At any given time, she would come to my house or I would go to her house with a new story in hand that one of us had written. Or perhaps we would write simultaneously, then read to the other what we had written. Of course, we also started a club about anything and everything – games, animals, school, whatever -- and the first on the agenda was to put in writing the rules and "bylaws" of whichever club we were putting into force!

During these young years, writing became a passion of mine, and I maintained a journal. My early journal writing was sporadic, though; sometimes every day, sometimes every month or so. I honestly don't remember if Paula kept a journal, but I wrote in one throughout my childhood – even though it was not always done on a daily basis. I also kept journals – sporadically – in my early adult years, but now in my latter years, I keep one on a daily basis. I also write in a "Writing Prompts" book as well as a prayer journal. What started out as fun for me when we were young, developed into the strong passion it is today.

A strong passion for Paula today is exercise, whether weights, aerobics, or yoga. Back in 1960, we never thought about exercise because of everything we did through bike riding and walking. We never walked to a gym – did they even have those then?? – or a rec center to exercise, but we did walk to the trampoline place near the amusement park and beach. For probably $.25 - $.50 per hour, we could jump on trampolines – located outside with the trampoline netting stretched over a hole in the cement. Within the fenced in area, there were probably ten trampoline nettings stretched over the holes in which kids could jump. We jumped, perspired, and jumped some more. By the time we could hardly jump another time, our hour was finished, and we dragged ourselves home. No, we didn't need to go to any exercise place – we had plenty with our walking, riding bicycles, or jumping on trampolines.

We also cheered constantly – making up our own – watching ourselves in the fender chrome of my daddy's car, parked in the driveway. I have to smile when I think of the two of us doing our cheers in the driveway, next to the back of the car so we could see ourselves in the fender chrome.

How many remember: "Strawberry shortcake, huckleberry pie! V-I-C-T-O-R-Y! Will we win it? Y-E-S!" I think I'm missing a line, but that was the general idea! And, of course, my all time favorite cheer that we made up ourselves, sometime in a musical sing-song voice: "I love peanut butter; creamy peanut butter; crunchy peanut butter too!" Wow – we exuded talent!! As I mentioned before, we went to Paula's school to watch the basketball games, but we were actually focused on the cheerleaders. What they did at the games, we brought back and attempted to perform while watching ourselves in the fender chrome of the car!

More exercise encompassed dancing. We danced in my garage, in my living room, and in my bedroom. I don't know why, but the dancing seemed to take place at my house and not hers. We attempted all the dance crazes, especially the Twist. Despite dancing the jitterbug, I think we pretty much perfected the Twist because we did it the most. A couple of years later, when we met everyone else in our "gang," our friend, Glenda, came to my house to show us a dance – I have no idea the name -- she had learned after she had been away from Norfolk on a vacation. To the song "Little Latin Lupe Lu," she bent over at the waist, shook her bottom, moved her hands back and forth with her thumbs up. Her face was contorted somewhat – perhaps trying for that sexy look. Paula and I watched, but I don't think it really caught on with us. We probably tried it, but that was about it – no more bent over, sexy dancing for us. Give us the Twist any day!

Another exercise for Paula and I was skating down Lenox Avenue. And skates were different back then. Definitely no in-line skating, but simple skates that hooked onto the sides of the shoes in the front and back, then tightened with a skate key. Done – down the street we went. Of course, we had sidewalks, but the cracks sometimes would cause difficulties, so it was better to skate in the street. We did skate to other places, but mainly, we stayed on Lenox Avenue.

When the day ended, it didn't stop for Paula and me – we had sleepovers. If we were in school, our sleepovers were only on the weekends; however, during the summer months, we had sleepovers as often as possible. Our sleepovers were almost an oxymoron – we did little sleeping! Instead, we listened to the radio and sang along with every song that was played. One specific D.J. – surprisingly, I can't remember his name -- played our favorite music all night, and even if we weren't having a sleepover, we still listened to him in our own bedrooms, falling asleep with the radio on.

At sleepovers, we tried new looks with our hair. Again, Paula always tried to have her hair straight rather than curly, and rolling it around orange juice cans was a favorite way to do so. This was not unusual, though, because Donna slept in large rollers or O.J. cans too "To get my smooth page boy look. That was fun!"

My hair was never long enough for the large

rollers or O.J. cans like Paula's and others, but bobby pins and pin curls was my style or rolling my hair on the brush rollers – oh, how they hurt to sleep on them – in a different way in which I was not used to doing. Some looks turned out quite well – others, not so much.

One thing we really didn't try much was putting on make-up. I don't believe either one of us thought about make-up and what we would look like with it on. Perhaps it was because neither of our moms had make-up other than lipstick around the house, or we just didn't like it. It's a mystery to me since I know girls in 2016 have tried make-up far younger than we were. I have to admit, though, we did try stuffing Kleenex in the tops of our blouses to see what that looked like, and that's all I'm going to say about that!

Of course, at our sleepovers we talked about boys, we told scary stories, we read and wrote, and we always ate! If we were at my house, we went downstairs and raided the refrigerator in the wee hours of the morning, eating the oddest food conglomerations we could find. That could be pickles with meats, olives with leftovers, peanut butter on something strange, anything out of the ordinary. Of course, we would always have something sweet to eat since my mother was known for her baking. It seemed she always had cakes, cookies, pies, or something that we could pile on our plates and take back upstairs.

The sweets, for me, happened at all times of the night and day! In fact, years later Paula said her dad told her I was a bad influence on her because of all the sweets I ate. Because of what I ate, it affected her since she ate it too. Paula's family seemed to be healthier than my family by eating vegetables, fruits, and few sweets. My family did eat veggies and fruits too, but we had an abundance of sweets around. Not only did my family have sweets around the house, but I was also able to buy them at the grocery store located across our big divided highway. The store was located across the "big divide" along with other stores such as the dentist's office, the drugstore, and the ice cream store – where Bubba rolled his newspapers.

Paula and I went to the grocery store, sometimes to get something for our parents, but most of the time to buy a candy bar – for five cents. And that five-cents candy bar was bigger and thicker than the candy bars that cost seventy-five cents today in 2016! We would also go to the drugstore, again perhaps to pick up something for our parents, but most likely to buy a Coke or a banana split, which we had to share because it was quite large! For forty-nine cents, the banana split was huge, and one person could not eat the entire goodie! If we went to the ice cream store, we bought an ice cream cone – for five cents. The game we always played with each other at the ice cream store: we had to buy the next flavor (since the last time we had bought a cone) listed on the menu hanging on the wall – whether we liked it or not. It is unbeknownst to me why that would have been a fun game to play, but we played every time we entered the ice cream store.

As Paula and I became older – no longer riding those great distances from our houses on bicycles – we went to parties. Those parties entailed dancing and hanging out with other teens; however, these teens were older than we were. They were also boys and girls with whom we didn't go to school. In fact, these many years later, we have talked on numerous occasions wondering how we met these older people and how we came to be at their parties when we were significantly younger than they were.

Recently, we actually drove to and sat in front of a house where we attended one of the parties. We even remembered it was in the basement, and we knew the name of the young man hosting the party. We still couldn't figure out how we had met him, and how we knew where he lived. It's another mystery for us, and, most likely, will never be answered.

From reading and writing to riding and walking, Paula and I did it all and enjoyed every minute of it. I can think of no one better with whom I would have wanted to spend my childhood and leave a legacy of memories than Paula Rapisardi O'Connor.

VIII
Saying Good-bye Is Never Easy

As most military families can relate, receiving orders can be traumatic for everyone – especially teen-agers. In the spring of 1964, my dad received his new orders – we were leaving Lenox Avenue -- when I was on the brink of turning fifteen years. Our destination was Key West, Florida. I was devastated at the news, and I cried almost every night after he told my mother and me. How could I leave my room? How could I leave Lenox Avenue and the best friends a girl could have? Above all, how could I leave the boy next door? No one could understand a heavy heart or a broken heart like I had when I received the news. I found it inconceivable that we would actually have to move.

It wasn't only military families, though, that received devastating news of a move. Donna's Dad applied for a job in another city from where her family lived and once he was hired, "Dad broke the news to us that we were leaving Knoxville. I was in the sixth grade, and I felt my world was crashing down around me. I had established wonderful friendships, loved my world at that time, and it was coming to an end."

Oh yes, saying good-bye is never easy. Nevertheless, my parents put the house up for sale – that unique house that we all cherished -- and not too long thereafter, people put an offer on it, and it was accepted. Sold! We started the process of moving. As a young girl, watching movers pack your most precious valuables was indescribably heartbreaking. Would they survive the move? Would they get lost? Would they look different away from my bedroom in the unique house on Lenox Avenue? A young girl's questions were endless and no answers were available. Or no answers that I wanted to hear.

When the movers were gone, and the house became a shell of itself, I made the trek upstairs to my room on that last day. I stood in my empty room and cried. It had been a room of thousands of memories with sleepovers, long talks, dressing up or dressing down, tears, and laughter.

Looking out the window toward the golf

course, I closed my eyes on visions of fairway walks, snowball fights, badminton competitions, and I cried. Walking to the other side of the room and looking out the window toward Lenox Avenue, I closed my eyes on visions of friends laughing, playing, singing, and I cried. The window fan – gone. The curtains – gone. My furniture – gone. Yes, indescribable pain.

I heard my name being called from downstairs. It was time.

Although we always knew moving could be at any time -- the plight of a military family -- it had left my mind completely while living on Lenox Avenue, and my thoughts were only of friends, fun, and Granby High School next year. Until my dad "dropped the bomb," I hadn't thought about moving away from Lenox Avenue. It seemed that life would go on in bliss and moving never occurred to me.

For me, I was in ninth grade, and six weeks was left to complete the year. I would have to transfer to a new school, first in Chattanooga, Tennessee, where my grandmother lived. We would be staying with her while my dad went on to Florida, checked in at his new base, and looked for a place for us to rent before we could live in base housing. Once I finished the ninth grade in Tennessee and leave newly made friends, I would have to transfer again to another new school in Florida, our final destination.

I heard my name being called with more emphasis again. It was definitely time now.

Complete sadness enveloped me as I took one last look at my room, slowly pulled the movable accordion wall closed, and walked to the top of the stairs. I looked into the bathroom and saw the window. Time fell away, and I could envision the four of us girls spying on all the guys. Tears welled and spilled over my cheeks.

I walked downstairs, stopping in the living room. I closed my eyes on its emptiness. So happy to have seen it for the first time; so sad to be leaving it on the day of departure. My mother, from the porch stoop, bade me to come, it was really time. She and I shut the door together on all the happiness I had known for the past few years.

Whether I had been there earlier or whether it was the first time that morning, we all found ourselves at Bubba's house. Paula was there, Bubba,

Bobby, and Mrs. Williams – I can remember no one else. Perhaps the others had said good-bye the night before, but I honestly don't remember other people being there on that fateful day.

Our car was packed with our suitcases, and we had to say our final good-byes. The heaviness I felt as I walked out of the Williams' house and down their porch steps was indescribable. Trying not to cry was not possible. As a teen-ager, it would have been embarrassing and humiliating to cry; nevertheless, the tears flowed freely. We hugged, we held on, and we cried. I don't know how my parents got me to the car, but I can remember sitting in the back seat and sobbing – the big ugly cry! Nothing pretty about it.

As my dad backed the car out of the driveway and slowly turned the corner, leaving Lenox Avenue behind, I looked out the back window. I saw my friends waving, my house, my beloved Lenox Avenue. It was now all in the distance and when we rounded the bend, I could no longer see everything I had cherished. I sobbed. No, I gulped, cried, and hiccupped until there was nothing left but the heartache.

I am sure my parents tired of my crying most of the way to Chattanooga, Tennessee; nevertheless, they never said a word. In fact, I think my mother, herself, shed a tear or two. The drive was simply somber and sad – no words were needed.

That day will live forever as a true pain in my heart; however, we all were able to write, and we did make a couple of telephone calls – no cell phones in the 1960s and long distance was expensive. I was able to return to Lenox Avenue on a visit when I was sixteen years old. I flew there from Florida by myself, and it was wonderful to see special friends once more. Need I say I was ecstatic to see a special someone, who had just turned twenty years old, and was no longer a boy. He was working – it could have been at a place called Sealtest -- and Paula and I went to his workplace to see him on the day I arrived. I still remember seeing him coming around the corner for the first time. His smile was captivating, and, at sixteen, my heart skipped a beat. I stayed with Paula the weeks that I was there, and saw Bubba every chance when he wasn't working. More cherished memories on Lenox Avenue.

While in and finishing high school, I carried his picture in my wallet, telling all my girlfriends, this was who I was going to marry. Of course, that was something Bubba had never said, but I always felt he would when the time was right.

Three years after leaving Norfolk, Virginia and my graduating from high school, my dad received orders to go to Sigonella, Sicily. My parents and I visited Lenox Avenue and the friends there, while driving from Florida to New York before boarding the ship for my dad's tour of duty overseas.

It was another cherished visit on Lenox Avenue. Bubba was now twenty-two and still handsome as ever. We were together constantly on that very short visit, and if he had said, "Let's run off before your parents leave for Sicily and get married," I would have said, "Yes!" In a heartbeat. He never said those words, and my parents and I left friends again through more sadness and more tears.

The last memory I have of his and my time on Lenox Avenue was the long distance phone call he asked me to make from New York – collect. I called, we talked, and after I hung up, I cried. It seemed to be intuition for me that things would never be the same after such a long time apart across the ocean and in another country.

That intuition was correct. Nevertheless, while I did lose touch with my first love, I never lost touch with my best friend. Paula and I have remained friends since we met fifty-five years ago. We often recall our days on Lenox Avenue and have driven down that sweet street pointing out the various houses and all the fun we had. When we do, it always brings back the good side of memory of two young girls and a very special someone.

The End.

Also By Marty Matthews

The (im)Perfect Plan

Momma's Deadly Secret

The Red Light Terror

Evil Desires

John: The Fisher of Men

Peter: A Messenger for Christ

Paul: A Messenger for Christ

Paul's 1st Epistle

About The Author

Marty Matthews is a former high school English teacher and has enjoyed writing for pleasure and fun all of her life. The (im)Perfect Plan was her first Christian murder mystery, and John: The Fisher of Men was her first novel based on the books of the Bible. She has since written 3 new murder mysteries and 3 more Bible books, those told in a very interesting novel form.

The mother of four girls, Marty lives with her husband, Fred, in Clarksville, Tennessee.

To know when Marty's next novel is coming, please sign up here to her private mailing list:
 http://eepurl.com/4PI9T

Marty on Facebook: Search Groups: Marty's Book Nook
https://www.facebook.com/groups/349535975211668/

Email: authormartymatthews@gmail.com

Made in the USA
Charleston, SC
04 October 2016